Postmaster General United States.

Postal savings banks

An argument in their favor, with appendices

Postmaster General United States.

Postal savings banks
An argument in their favor, with appendices

ISBN/EAN: 9783337115197

Printed in Europe, USA, Canada, Australia, Japan

Cover: Foto ©Andreas Hilbeck / pixelio.de

More available books at **www.hansebooks.com**

51ST CONGRESS, ⎰   SENATE.   ⎰ MIS. DOC.
  2d Session. ⎰   ⎰ No. 91.

POSTAL SAVINGS BANKS.

AN ARGUMENT IN THEIR FAVOR

BY

THE POSTMASTER-GENERAL,

WITH

APPENDICES:

1. DRAFT OF BILL TO ESTABLISH POSTAL SAVINGS BANKS AND ENCOURAGE SMALL SAVINGS.
2. INTERESTING DETAILS OF POSTAL SAVINGS BANK SYSTEMS IN FOREIGN COUNTRIES.
3. OPINIONS OF FORMER POSTMASTERS-GENERAL.
4. SUMMARY OF THE EFFORTS TO PROVIDE LEGISLATION ON THE SUBJECT OF POSTAL SAVINGS BANKS.
5. RESOLUTION OF THE UNITED STATES SENATE TO INQUIRE AS TO THE FEASIBILITY AND ADVISABILITY OF ENACTMENT OF LAW CREATING POSTAL SAVINGS BANKS.
6. SENTIMENT OF THE PUBLIC PRESS.

FEBRUARY 2, 1891.—Presented by Mr. MITCHELL, referred to the Committee on Post-Offices and Post-Roads, and ordered to be printed.

WASHINGTON:
GOVERNMENT PRINTING OFFICE.
1891.

POSTAL SAVINGS BANKS.

AN ARGUMENT IN THEIR FAVOR BY THE POSTMASTER-GENERAL.

OFFICE OF THE POSTMASTER-GENERAL,
Washington, D. C., February 26, 1891.

DEAR SIR: Referring to your letter of December 17, asking for information in relation to postal savings banks, with such facts or statistics as I could obtain, I beg to lay before you my views on this subject, with certain details of the postal savings systems in Sweden, Great Britain, Austria, Belgium, the Netherlands, France, Russia, and Italy, and also the opinions of some of my predecessors in this office, and a summary of the legislation that has been attempted since 1873 up to the present time.

I have also added, as a suggestion to you and your committee, a bill which I think covers my views as to the legislation needed. The resolution of the Senate which calls out this paper is also returned herewith.

PUBLIC SENTIMENT FAVORS POSTAL SAVINGS BANKS.

Savings banks are the outgrowth of a popular desire for some safe place for the deposit of money, where it will add to itself interest instead of lying idle and useless. The public sentiment of our day, as voiced through the press, is almost unanimous in advocating the institution of savings banks under the patronage of the Government. Charitable institutions of various sorts are united in pressing upon the public attention and upon legislators the need of such banks. Financiers who have sought for channels of benevolence have established various private affairs for the savings of the poor, and of the so-called working classes.

There seems to be nothing to mar the unanimity of the sentiment among all classes and conditions in favor of this beneficent plan, whereby the faith of all the people is pledged in financial transactions to the security of the individual. These efforts have found various outlets. One started in a committee on the elevation of the poor in their homes, a committee of the State Charities Aid Association of the State of New York, and the chief motive which influenced that committee was the avowed need of some form of depository which would be protected against loss by an unquestionable guaranty.

This movement is entitled to more than passing notice because it is averred that it is based upon a wide-spread knowledge of the actual wants of the poorer classes of society derived from personal intercourse with them. In our day and in our country the poor man and the workingman (there are comparatively few very poor and most of our people

3

are workers) need no patronizing. They do not want to be helped so much as to be shown how to help themselves, or, rather, to be more limited, to be afforded proper modes of helping themselves. They do not need charity or government aid or paternalism; all that they ask for is absolute security.

The inculcation of the habit of saving leads to better citizenship. Every depositor in a Government bank has, so to speak, a stake in the country ; he is therefore against disorder and anarchy and our institutions are safer. His family is better provided for. The doctrine has been recorded in previous discussions upon this subject, that whatever can be as well done by private enterprise as by the Government should never be entered upon by the latter, and the committee of Congress at that time having the matter in charge expressly disclaimed any purpose of superseding or interfering with sound institutions then or thereafter organized by private enterprise. The opinion was strongly expressed, however, that private enterprise alone does not and can not in this respect meet the necessities of the industrious poor in any country, and least of all the United States.

The prime requisite to induce methodical saving is the privilege of depositing very small sums, and no less important, as has been stated, is the guaranty of undoubted security. The inducement to hold out the former is lacking to individuals or corporations, who, for the sake of larger gains, resort to broader fields for their enterprise. As for the latter, none but the Government can give it. While the conditions are not precisely the same, it will be useful to look to the experience of other countries in this regard and to observe with what success these depositories under the care of the Government have met.

THE EXPERIENCE OF OTHER COUNTRIES—GREAT BRITAIN.

The discussion began in Great Britain as early as in 1807 and was continued by philanthropists in parliament for 54 years against bitter opposition from the partisans of private savings banks until 1861. On May 17 of that year an act was passed entitled " An act to grant additional facilities for depositing small savings at interest, with the security of the Government for the due repayment thereof. "

It is noteworthy that after the lapse of 15 years the private savings banks had increased their capital by more than $10,000,000, which was the best answer to those who had opposed the scheme on the ground that they would ruin private savings banks. The fact that they have met the anticipations of their founders and have proved beneficial even beyond expectations, is best shown by the statistics of the latest report of the British postmaster-general, that for the year ended March 31, 1890, wherein it appears that the number of post-office savings banks is 9,353, the total amount standing to the credit of depositors is £62,999,620 (at $4.87 to the pound, equivalent to $306,808,149), and that in England and Wales the number of accounts was 1 to every 7 of population; in Scotland 1 to every 25, and in Ireland 1 to every 25, an average in the whole United Kingdom of 1 depositor to every 8 inhabitants, with an average balance to the credit of each depositor of nearly £14 ($68.18). The increase in the amount to the credit of depositors for the single year ending December 31, 1889, was nearly £4,500,000 ($21,915,000), and the interest credited to them that one year was nearly £1,500,000 ($7,305,000).

There were as high as 55,000 depositors in a single day, while the greatest number of withdrawals in a single day was 18,499.

CANADA.

In 1867 there were in two of the provinces of Canada regularly organized savings banks, with deposits amounting to $3,489,000. In that year a proposition was introduced in the Canadian legislature to establish post-office savings banks, popular attention having been attracted by the success of the British post-office banks. The measure received but little attention, and was the subject of but little comment and no hostile criticism.

It is stated that the discussion was confined to fixing the limit to the maximum deposits of a single person, the object being twofold: first, to exclude from the benefits of the Government banks any but the wage-earning classes, and, second, to protect the Canadian chartered banks. There was the fear which has been apparent in the history of the subject in other countries, that deposits in private institutions would seek the post-office banks; but after 16 years' experience the comptroller of the Canadian system stated that the banking institutions of Canada were satisfied that they had little to fear in this respect from the post-office savings banks. The system went into effect in Canada on the 1st of April, 1868, at 81 offices, the deposits amounting for the year ending June 30, 1869, to $856,814.26. For the year ended June 30, 1889, the number of depositors was 113,123, and the aggregate amount to the credit of depositors, $22,413,123.

An interesting inquiry made in Canada in 1885 disclosed the fact that the most largely interested class in the postal savings banks were farmers, whose deposits comprised over one-third of the whole; that the deposits of married women were the next most numerous, being nearly one-fifth of the whole. Next to these in order came mechanics, single women, laborers, widows, clerks, and tradesmen, while professional men are near the foot of the list.

FRANCE.

The establishment of the postal savings banks in France was authorized in 1881, and on the 31st of December, 1888, the number of open accounts was 1,129,984, and the amount to the credit of the depositors $51,490,200.

AUSTRIA.

On the 31st of December, 1889, the number of depositors in Austria was 719,431 and the amount of deposits $8,511,250, while in Hungary the depositors numbered on December 31, 1888, 129,887, with accounts to their credit aggregating $1,412,685. At the close of the same year in Belgium there were 593,979 depositors, with an aggregate balance of $48,699,644; and the astonishing statement is added that in this country the number of depositors trebled in 8 years and the amount of deposits doubled in the same period.

THE NETHERLANDS.

The Netherlands had $5,666,260 to the credit of 201,763 depositors, and Sweden held $746,502 to the credit of 152,016 depositors, 59 per centum of whom were minors. The postal savings banks were sanctioned recently in Russia; and Germany, it is believed, is now the only one of the great powers of Europe which does not possess this system.

AUSTRALASIAN COLONIES.

The Australasian colonies have followed in the footsteps of the mother country, and south Australia has 64,320 depositors, with credits amounting to $9,234,722; Queensland, 43,003 depositors, with $7,849,836; New Zealand, 84,488 depositors, with balances amounting to $9,975,907.

OTHER COUNTRIES.

Even the Cape of Good Hope has 15,505 patrons of this system, who possess in the aggregate credits amounting to $1,562,437. British Guiana has 136 depositors with $2,279 to their credit, and the British comptroller of savings banks states that some of the deposits bear evident traces of having been unearthed in the literal sense of the word, proving the need which some thrifty persons had experienced of a safe place of deposit. In Ceylon the system was established as late as 1885, yet in 1887 there were 144 offices, with 6,685 depositors, and deposits amounting to 129,175 rupees. The system is stated to have proved a boon to the poorer population, the most gratifying feature being that the best customers are the Singhalese.

To come nearer home there is a post-office savings bank in the Hawaiian Kingdom, which was inaugurated June 1, 1886, and in 3 years the depositors numbered 2,641 and the deposits amounted to $885,960. The funds are employed on public improvements.

For convenience of reference a table is here given, showing the condition of postal savings banks in the principal European countries at the beginning of the year 1889:

Names of countries and year of the establishment of the postal savings banks.	Number of depositors on the 31st December, 1888.	Deposits.			Repayments.		
		Number.	Aggregate amount.	Average amount.	Number.	Aggregate amount.	Average amount.
Austria (1883):							
Saving	655,335	1,147,917	$7,728,058.14	$6.75	356,184	$6,625,402.43	$18.20
Checks	14,296	4,281,780	310,765,131.79	72.58	1,238,144	310,111,655.40	2.51
Belgium (1869)	392,316	831,489	11,766,469.65	14.15	203,530	8,310,548.03	40.83
Canada (1868)	108,409	160,085	8,078,245.25	50.50	83,081	7,830,114.22	94.25
France (1882), including Algeria and Tunis	1,120,984	1,455,780	32,677,370.98	22.44	536,665	25,710,535.92	47.91
Hungary (February 1, 1886) ...	120,887	431,108	1,734,729.25	4.02	118,654	1,355,229.98	11.42
Italy (1876)	1,710,943	2,040,937	33,313,152.35	16.32	1,162,234	30,160,894.74	29.95
Netherlands (1881) .	201,763	445,799	3,762,317.61	8.48	131,969	2,745,164.84	20.67
United Kingdom (1861)	4,220,927	7,540,625	92,662,606.33	12.28	2,633,808	76,858,181.95	29.18
Sweden	174,327	212,206	877,875.36	4.22	41,191	418,863.46	10.17

SUMMARY.

Names of countries and year of the establishment of the postal savings banks.	Aggregate amount of the sums due the depositors.	Average due each depositor.	Number of depositors per 1,000 inhabitants.	Aggregate of the sums due per 1,000 inhabitants.
Austria (1883):				
Saving	$7,236,410.20	$11.04	29	$327.55
Checks	136,472,448.09	954.63	0.64	616.15
Belgium (1869)	27,491,933.83	70.07	65	4,559.16
Canada (1868)	22,581,626.67	208.44	23	4,599.09
France (1882), including Algeria and Tunis	51,490,200.19	44.66	25.70	1,174.60
Hungary (February 1, 1886)	1,412,685.30	10.88	7.80	85.61
Italy (1876)	49,516,486.07	28.94	60	1,739.76
Netherlands (1881)	5,666,260.56	27.98	47.20	895.73
United Kingdom (1861)	284,794,877.70	77.47	111	7,488.01
Sweden	1,301,300.94	7.46	37	275.03

PRIVATE SAVINGS BANKS DO NOT MEET THE WANTS OF THE PEOPLE.

1.—THEY DO NOT AFFORD ADEQUATE PROTECTION.

It is not hard to show that private institutions do not meet the wants of all the people. In the first place they do not afford adequate protection to those who are not able to protect themselves. In the second place they are not open at all times and seasons, nor at convenient hours, nor for long-continued periods; they are not situated at convenient points; in a word they are not designed or adapted to the convenience of our population, nor have they either the incentive of philanthropy or of gain to induce them to become so.

Recently in the prosecution of this matter, which had concerned me for some time prior to the introduction in your body of the resolution to which this aims to be an answer, I had undertaken an inquiry for the purpose of ascertaining in what manner and to what extent private banks and savings institutions were authorized, restricted, or controlled by legislation in the various States of the Union. To this end I caused inquiries to be addressed to the governors of the various States, and here make acknowledgment of the uniform courtesy of these officers, in responding with the fullest information at their command. My purpose here is to sift the replies received and give only the gist of such as have direct bearing upon the question of the security afforded by such private concerns throughout the various States, to the savings or investment deposits of our people. I shall make the summary in as few words as possible, giving merely the substance of the answer received by the Post-Office Department, to wit:

INADEQUATE STATE LAWS.

South Carolina.—The banks in the State are governed by the terms of their charter alone.

Maryland.—The laws are very meager on the subject. The affairs of the concern to be examined annually by a committee appointed by the directors, and report published, and the bank subject to examination by the State treasurer at any time.

Minnesota.—There are no laws directly relating to private banks, the attempted legislation of 1887 in regard to such banks having failed to become laws for lack of the constitutional majority in the legislature.

Nevada.—We have no officer that has anything to do with banks to refer the matter to. (Meaning my inquiry.)

Mississippi.—The private or savings banks may be conducted by individuals or may be incorporated under the general laws of the State. There is no restriction as to capital or ownership of property.

Kentucky.—We have no general banking law, but all bank charters are granted by the legislature, with their especial privileges, an evil which we trust will be remedied by the constitutional convention now in session in this city (Frankfort).

Michigan.—There is no law governing private banks in this State.

South Dakota.—We have no banking law. Banks like all other corporations are allowed under our general incorporation laws, and they are not subject to any limitation other than would apply to any moneyed corporation. Banks may also be operated without incorporating. The latter are not under any State supervision. The former are subject to supervision as follows. (Here follows a statement as to the public examiner being authorized to visit each corporation once a year and ascertain its condition.) The examiner has but little power under the law, yet the examination and publication of the annual reports has a wholesome effect upon the banks. (Here follow certain provisions of the criminal code, restrictive of the operations of the banks.)

Oregon.—Private banks may be incorporated under the general laws of the State, but there is no legislation whatever especially regulating the affairs of such banks or authorizing any officer to inquire into their condition. The only exception to this statement is the power of the assessors to make the usual inquiry respecting taxable property.

Texas.—The creation of corporations for banking purposes is inhibited by the constitution of this State. We have no statutes relating to private banks.   .   ,

Kansas.—Private banks are not controlled or restricted by the legislation of this State. Savings banks are controlled by legislation only so far as to compel them to obtain a charter, file a certificate of incorporation, giving name and amount of the stock of each shareholder, and make sworn semiannual statements of their financial condition. The business affairs of a savings bank in this State are controlled entirely by its board of directors.

FAILURES OF PRIVATE BANKS.

That private banking institutions do not afford adequate security to depositors is most clearly demonstrated by the statistics at the command of the Government, showing the failure of private banking firms and contrasting these failures in their extent and effect with the losses incurred through the insolvency of national banks. These statistics are comparatively limited, but such as they are they constitute such strong proof of mismanagement and recklessness of concerns free from adequate governmental or State restraint as to furnish the best evidence upon the point desired in this discussion to be emphasized.

From the beginning of the national banking system until 1879, a period of 16 years, only 81 national banks had become insolvent, and the estimated losses all told were $6,240,189. It is stated in the publications on the subject that 55 banks operating under systems in vogue prior to the national banking system, failed in the single year 1841, with an aggregate capital of over $67,000,000. And it is also recorded that in nearly every instance the entire capital of the banks which failed was lost. The losses incident to three or four failures of private banking firms prior to 1879 were equal to the total losses which had up to that time occurred under the national system.· During 3 years ending January 1, 1879, the failures of State and savings banks and private banks in 23 States numbered 210, with losses amounting to $32,616,661.

The average annual losses to creditors by the insolvency of national banks during 16 years prior to 1879 was $390,012, while that occasioned by the failure of banks other than national was for 3 years prior to 1879 not less than $10,872,220 per annum. The report of the Comptroller of the Currency for 1879 shows that in the States of Ohio and Illinois alone the losses in 3 years through the failure of State, savings, and private banks and bankers aggregated over $8,000,000, of which about $2,000,000 were in Ohio and about $6,000,000 in Illinois, the total losses in these two States being greater by $1,798,913 than the total losses to creditors by all the national bank failures which have ever occurred.

In 8 years the losses to creditors through the failures of national banks in the cities of New York and Brooklyn were $91,000, while the losses by savings banks in the same two cities for a corresponding period were nearly $4,500,000.

The Treasury Department has received reports of the condition of 860 savings banks in thirty-five States and Territories, and the results approximately cover the whole field. Of the 860 savings banks, 235 are stock associations, with deposits of $192,635,519. The remaining 625 are mutual savings associations having deposits aggregating $1,268,309,742. There are also unofficial reports from 61 savings banks in a number of States and Territories where no provision is made for securing reports or for examination of banks organized under their authority and the deposits in them are stated to be $89,078,695.

2.—SAVINGS BANKS NOT NUMEROUS IN MANY SECTIONS OF THE COUNTRY.

Six hundred and thirty-seven of the 921 savings banks are purely mutual; the other 284 are stock savings banks. It is easy to understand why private savings banks do not meet the public needs in another respect, when it is stated that of the 637 mutual savings banks, all but 11 are located in the New England States, and in New York, New Jersey, Pennsylvania, Delaware, Maryland, and the District of Columbia. These 11 are distributed as follows: In Ohio, 4; in Indiana, 5; in Wisconsin, 1; and in West Virginia, 1. The aggregate deposits of the mutual savings banks amount to $1.336,001,150, and the average rate of interest paid to depositors is about 3.8 per cent.

The savings deposits in the 284 stock savings banks amount to $188,- 843,356. Two hundred and nineteen of these banks are in the Western States and Territories, 11 in Vermont, 7 in Maryland, 4 in Pennsylvania, and the few remaining, only 43 in all, are distributed as follows: 4 in North Carolina, 12 in Georgia, 1 in Louisiana, 1 in West Virginia, 13 in South Carolina, 2 in Florida, and 10 in Tennessee.

The following table, the figures in which are taken from the last report of the Comptroller of the Currency, is a comprehensive statement of the more interesting items in regard to private savings banks:

States.	Number of banks.	Savings deposits.	Number of depositors.	Average deposit.
Mutual savings banks, official.				
Maine	55	$43,977,085	132,192	$332.68
New Hampshire	72	65,727,019	159,782	411.35
Vermont	20	14,757,287	51,398	287.12
Massachusetts	177	332,723,688	1,029,694	323.13
Rhode Island	38	60,479,707	127,898	472.88
Connecticut	86	110,370,962	294,890	374.27
New York	124	550,066,657	1,420,997	387.10
New Jersey	26	30,946,878	117,853	262.58
Maryland	16	35,603,591	121,975	291.89
District of Columbia	1	1,303,717	12,534	104.01
Ohio	4	19,207,004	47,294	406.10
Indiana	5	3,078,608	13,062	235.69
Wisconsin	1	67,539	615	109.81
Total	625	1,268,309,742	3,530,190	....
Mutual savings banks, unofficial.				
Pennsylvania	9	63,957,341	216,757	295.06
Delaware	2	3,603,531	16,000	225.22
West Virginia	1	130,536	2,371	55.06
Total	12	67,691,408	235,128	....

States.	Number of banks.	Savings deposits.	Number of depositors.	Average deposit.
Stock savings banks, official.				
Vermont	11	4, 573, 277	14, 361	318. 45
Maryland	7	320, 520	1, 839	174. 29
North Carolina	4	209, 363	4, 043	51. 78
Georgia	12	2, 637, 648	43, 876	60. 12
Louisiana	1	1, 182, 482	3, 421	345. 65
Illinois	15	11, 193, 401	42, 170	265, 43
Michigan	67	27, 237, 582	124, 664	218. 49
Iowa	59	16, 336, 787	44, 838	364. 35
Minnesota	8	5, 845, 209	21, 017	278. 12
California	37	98, 442, 007	124, 967	787. 74
New Mexico	1	109, 407	418	261. 74
Utah	7	1, 512, 580	9, 881	153. 08
Washington	6	523, 129	5, 634	92. 85
Total	235	170, 123, 392	401, 129	
Stock savings banks, unofficial.				
Pennsylvania	4	$1, 625, 602	4, 856	$334. 76
West Virginia	1	169, 692	3, 859	44. 00
South Carolina	13	3, 274, 440	21, 855	149. 82
Florida	2	85, 462	467	183. 00
Tennessee	10	1, 650, 940	13, 577	121. 60
Ohio	10	8, 936, 259	26, 041	343. 16
Montana	1	344, 599	3, 233	106. 59
Nebraska	8	2, 632, 970	18, 558	141. 19
Total	49	18, 719, 964	92, 446	
Grand total	921	1, 524, 844, 506	4, 258, 803	358. 04

STRONG ADVOCACY IN THE PAST.

The question of postal savings banks has been advocated in Congress ever since the first forceful discussion in Postmaster-General Creswell's Reports of 1871, 1872, and 1873, for in the latter year Mr. Maynard, of Tennessee, then a member of the House of Representatives, afterwards Postmaster-General, introduced a carefully drawn bill to establish and maintain a national savings depository as a branch of the Post-Office Department. This was followed at short intervals by other bills in both the House and Senate, in the years 1877, 1878, 1881, 1882, and 1886, all substantially drafted upon the same models and all having the same object in view.

A summary of these bills is printed in the appendix, together with extracts from a report on the subject heretofore made by a Congressional committee, to wit, that of Mr. Lacey, from the Committee on the Post-Office and Post-Roads, of the House, February 21, 1882. This report is of peculiar interest in this connection and at this time, in view of the circumstance that Mr. Lacey is now the Comptroller of the Currency, and that his views, as one of the chief financial officers of the Government, are entitled to the most serious consideration.

THE PRESS FAVORS POSTAL SAVINGS BANKS.

Added to all this, from an executive and legislative standpoint, there is the universal sentiment of the public press of the country seeking continually at the hands of the Government the establishment of these institutions as an incentive to thrift and a remedy for the ills of extravagance. There are scarcely two sides to the question, from their standpoint, as will be seen by reference to the appendix, where are set out the editorial utterances of the leading newspapers of the country.

THE OBSTACLES HERETOFORE.

It may be wondered, with all this array of advocacy uniformly and strongly in favor of the establishment of postal savings banks as a branch of the Post-Office Department, why the measure seemed never to make substantial headway. I have studied the question with much care, and the reason seems to be plain. There has come before legislators, at each periodical discussion of the subject, a mountain of obstacle in the way of providing as to what disposal shall be made of the sums received from depositors. That they would be enormous in amount can not be doubted. Great Britain with its population of 35,241,482, already has over $300,000,000 in its postal savings banks. The United States, with almost double the population and with greater possibilities afforded to its thrifty artisans to accumulate small savings, would with scarce a doubt be confronted with the problem of how best to take care of a much larger sum than $300,000,000 and possibly as much as $500,000,000. If it were but a question of housing this money in vaults, so that it would be safe from burglary, fire, or casualty of other description, the matter of security could be simply enough solved, but it would be against public policy to withdraw from circulation and lock up in the Treasury vaults such an enormous sum of money.

What must be done is to make this money earn interest, so that it may pay the running expenses of a savings-bank system, and at least a small rate of interest to depositors. This point was commented upon in one of the pamphlets issued by the State Charities Aid Association of the State of New York, in 1887, which proposed a measure providing that no interest should be promised upon the money deposited, and they state that nothing more is asked for by the laboring classes themselves than a safe place in which they may put their small savings. Said they:

The request is made simply for opportunity to deposit their savings in the Treasury of the United States, either with or without interest as the public finances may justify.

And they pathetically add:

Strange as it may seem, there are men to-day in Congress who would deny even this little boon asked for, for use of the United States Treasury vaults for the safe-keeping of the earnings of the poor.

They even attempted to meet the objection as to the withdrawal from circulation of the sum of the deposits, by saying that—

No man of sense will long allow $200 or $300 to lie idle where it is drawing no interest; that the money is as much withdrawn from circulation now as it would be then, for it is stored in old stockings and bureau drawers, the difference being that it is now exposed to theft.

This scarcely goes to the merit of the question. It is doubtful whether the United States could successfully deviate from the practice of other countries, which uniformly pay a rate of interest, whether it be large or small. The United States must, therefore, before it can receive these sums from depositors, have a certain prospective use for the money. Can that use be found? Herein lies the whole problem of the post-office savings banks, and herein also lies the only obstacle which heretofore has successfully prevented their establishment.

European countries are not met with this problem. They have their varying indebtednesses not likely to be materially reduced, perhaps for centuries, possibly in some cases guarantied to be permanent indebtednesses. It is not so with us. The policy of the Government since the creation of its tremendous war debt has been to pay off its obligations as rapidly as its revenues would permit.

WHAT SHALL BE DONE WITH THE MONEY IN THE ABSENCE OF A
PERMANENT NATIONAL DEBT ?

There is no sentiment at this day which would support the creation
of a permanent indebtedness even for a sentimental object which would
result in lasting good to the great body of the people.   It has thus been
brought about that the debt incident to the prosecution of the war of
the rebellion, which reached its maximum on August 31, 1865, and
amounted at that date to $2,844,649,626, or, leaving out the non-interest-
bearing obligations, to $2,383,033,315, has been discharged until to-
day it amounts to less than $700,000,000. This debt is composed of
$64,000,000 of 4½ per cent. bonds, $568,000,000 of 4 per cent. bonds,
and $64,000,000 of 6 per cent. bonds, the latter being known as Pacific
Railroad bonds. The 4½ per cent. bonds mature during the current
year. The Pacific bonds mature from 1895 to 1899. The remainder,
which constitutes the great bulk of the interest-bearing debt of the
United States at this time, absolutely and wholly matures in 1907, or
within 17 years.

It is therefore a serious matter to think of receiving perhaps
$500,000,000 from depositors in the postal savings banks, with the
prospect of the entire extinguishment of the National debt within that
brief period, and the consequent total want of interest-bearing securities guarantied upon the faith and credit of the Government, in which
to invest such moneys. There seems to be but one view upon the
question of the extinguishment of the National debt.

The Comptroller of the Currency says in 1889 :

The rapid extinguishment of our National debt which has taken place since the
close of the late war has given the United States greater influence in its intercourse
with other nations than any exhibition of strength which could have been made in
the way of organizing armies, building navies, or constructing coast defenses.

The Secretary of the Treasury, in his last report to Congress upon the
state of the finances, makes some pertinent observations upon the subject of the surplus revenue and the consequent purchase of the bonds
and their application to the sinking fund. He says that to prevent an un-
due accumulation of money in the Treasury and consequent commercial
stringency, only two methods are open to the Department, namely, to
deposit the money in the national banks or continue the purchase of
United States bonds on such terms as they could be obtained. The
former method was deemed to be unwise, and the bond purchases continued. On account of the rapidly diminishing supply of United States
bonds on the market, and of the fact that the sudden and great increase
in the surplus compelled the immediate purchase of large quantities, it
became very difficult to obtain them in sufficient amounts and at fair
prices. The Secretary here interposes a brief statement of the succes-
sive and labored attempts taken by him to dispose of the constantly
accumulating surplus of the public money by purchases becoming
more and more difficult of the interest-bearing bonds. His recital has
so strong a bearing upon the point under discussion that part of it is
quoted here:

There were outstanding on June 30, 1889, United States interest-bearing bonds, issued under the refunding act, in the amount of $815,734,350, of which $676,095,350
were 4 percents, and $139,639,000 4½ percents. During the fiscal year 1890 there
were purchased of these bonds $73,924,500 4's and $30,623,250 4½ per cents, and there
remained outstanding June 30, 1890, $602,193,500 4's, including $21,650 issued for refunding certificates, and $109,015,750 4½ per cents. Of the bonds so purchased there
were applied to the sinking-fund for the fiscal year 1890 $27,695,600 4's and $12,136,750
4½ percents, the residue being ordinary redemptions of the debt.

During this period the Secretary was able to purchase United States bonds at constantly decreasing prices, so that at the end of the fiscal year 1890 the Government was paying for 4 per cent. bonds 7 per cent. less than at the beginning of that period, and for 4½ per cent. bonds 4½ per cent. less; but the diminished supply of bonds held for sale, together with the lower prices which were being paid, had been gradually curtailing the Government purchases, and soon after the beginning of the present fiscal year the growing surplus and the prospective needs of the country made it advisable that steps be taken to obtain more free offerings of bonds to the Government.

Accordingly, on July 19, 1890, a circular was published rescinding that under which purchases had been made since April 17, 1888, and inviting new proposals, to be considered July 24, for the sale of the two classes of bonds before mentioned. Under this circular there were offered on the day prescribed $6,402,350 4 percents and $594,550 4½ percents, at prices varying from 121.763 to 128.263 for 4's, and from 103¼ to 104.40 for 4½'s, of which there were purchased all the 4 percents offered at 124 or less, amounting to $6,381,350, and all the 4½'s offered at 103¼, or less, amounting to $584,550. As the amount obtained on this day was less than the Government desired to purchase, the provisions of the circular were extended, with the result that further purchases were made, amounting in the aggregate to $9,652,500 4's and $706, 450 4½ percents.

It was soon apparent that these purchases were inadequate to meet existing conditions; therefore, on August 19, the Department gave notice that 4½ per cent bonds would be redeemed with interest to and including May 31, 1891; and two days later the circular of August 21 was published, inviting the surrender for redemption of $20,000,000 of those bonds, upon condition of the prepayment after September 1, 1890, of all the interest to and including August 31, 1891, on the bonds so surrendered. Under this circular there were redeemed $20,060,700 4½ percent.

Notwithstanding the disbursements resulting from purchases and redemptions of bonds under the circulars of July 19 and August 21, the industrial and commercial interests of the country required that large additional amounts should be at once returned to the channels of trade. Accordingly, a circular was published August 30, 1890, inviting the surrender of an additional 20,000,000 of 4½ per cents. upon the same terms as before. This was followed by another, dated September 6, inviting holders of the 4 per cent. bonds to accept prepayment of interest on those bonds to July 1, 1891, a privilege which was subsequently extended to the holders of currency 6's. Under this circular of August 30 there were redeemed $18,678,100 4½ per cent. bonds, and under that of September 6 there was prepaid on the 4 per cent. bonds and currency 6's interest amounting to $12,009,951.50.

These prepayments of interest are expressly authorized by section 3699 of the Revised Statutes. They were deemed expedient because of the disposition of the holders of bonds to demand exorbitant prices for them.

The amount of public money set free within 75 days by these several disbursements was nearly $76,660,000, and the net gain to circulation was not less than $45,000,000, yet the financial conditions made further prompt disbursements imperatively necessary. A circular was therefore published September 13, 1890, inviting proposals, to be considered on the 17th, for the sale, to the Government, of 16,000,000 of 4 per cent. bonds. The offerings under this circular amounted to $35,514,900, of which $17,071,150 were offered at 126¾, or less, and were accepted.

It should be stated that there is no saving of interest on the 4½ per cent. bonds redeemed under the circulars of August 21 and 30, since all the interest on those bonds to September 1, 1891, the date on which they become redeemable, has been prepaid, and that the reduction in the annual interest charge on the same bonds takes effect only from that date.

Another circular inviting the surrender of 4½ per cent. bonds for redemption, with interest to and including August 31, 1891, was published October 9, 1890. The amount surrendered under that circular during the month of October was $3,203,100.

The total amount of 4 and 4½ per cent. bonds purchased and redeemed since March 4, 1889, is $211,832,450, and the amount expended therefor is $246,620,741.72. The reduction in the annual interest charge by reason of these transactions is $8,967,609.75, and the total saving of interest is $51,576,706.01.

It will be seen from the above statement that during the 3¼ months, from July 19 to November 1, 1890, over $99,000,000 were disbursed in payment for bonds and interest.

There are many grave objections to the accumulation of a large surplus in the Treasury, and especially to the power which the control of such surplus gives to the Secretary. I am sure those objections appeal to no one with so much force as to the head of the Department upon whom rests the difficult and delicate responsibility of its administration.

HOW SHALL POSTAL SAVINGS FUNDS BE DISPOSED OF?

It has been proposed in several of the measures heretofore before
the Congress to invest the funds received on deposit in postal savings
banks either in interest-bearing securities of the United States, or in
any interest-bearing securities guaranteed by the United States, or
finally, in the most approved State securities obtainable at the time. I
have shown that the interest-bearing securities of the United States
are not available now for distribution of the accumulating surplus revenues, and that investment of savings-bank funds therein seems to be
out of the question. I do not believe that legislative sanction can be
obtained for the investment of funds in the bonds of the various States,
for the reason that there is present in the public mind the vivid recol-
lection of the repudiation by several of the States of their bonded indebtedness, and of the protracted litigation in others on the same subject.

THE PLAN RECOMMENDED.

I have already recommended a plan which I believe to be feasible,
and it contemplates the establishment of postal savings banks, first, in
States which have no laws governing private savings banks, and,
second, upon suitable petition of a considerable number of the residents of any locality, in any other States.

While the experience of several foreign countries has shown that
private savings banks are not antagonized by similar government institutions, the plan I propose removes objection on that score by providing that the rate of interest shall be at least one-half of 1 per cent.
less than the average rate paid within a State by private bankers to
depositors.

I have recommended that all the postal savings funds received within
a State be placed on deposit with the national banks of that State, in
such amounts and at such rates of interest as the Secretary of the
Treasury shall prescribe. There is thus provided a channel for the
disposal of the money which will place it rapidly in circulation in the
locality from which it is gathered for original deposit in the postal
savings banks, and through which it will unquestionably earn a sufficient sum to pay expenses and a moderate rate of interest to depositors.

And, finally, I have suggested that deposits of postal savings funds
shall be declared by special enactment preferred claims against the
national banks holding them. I do not think any better security offers
itself in the present state of the country and I believe it will be adequate.

OTHER SUGGESTIONS.

There are other suggestions which will occur to the thoughtful mind
as to channels for placing the funds of the depositors. One of them is
in the direction of greater and much needed expenditures for public,
and particularly for post-office buildings. I find that from 1870 to 1890,
inclusive, there has been an average expenditure per annum, on account
of public buildings, to be used chiefly for custom-houses, post-offices,
and court-houses, the large sum of $3,217,253.00, a total in 21 years of
$67,562,306.86. There could scarcely be conceived a better investment
for the public funds than to place them in such Government real estate,
which by the very act of its acquirement by the United States, would
become of enhanced value and would continue to increase in value year

by year. It would, moreover, give to the people that conception of security which always surrounds investments in real property. There is not only the outlet in the way of ordinary expenditures to be taken into account, but there are the further large needs of the country at this time to be considered, particularly in the direction of additional accommodations for post-offices in numerous towns and cities.

On December 4, 1889, Mr. Vest introduced in the Senate a bill to provide for the erection of public buildings for post-offices in towns and cities where the post-offices receipts for 3 years preceding have exceeded $3,000 annually. This bill provides for the construction from time to time of buildings for the accommodation of all Presidential post-offices, the annual gross receipts of which for 3 years preceding shall have exceeded the sum of $3,000, said buildings to be fairly distributed among the several States and Territories. It also provides that the cost of no such building shall exceed $25,000, and stipulates that the site of every building shall be of such size as to afford a clear space of not less than 50 feet in extent on each side of and beyond the limits of the building, obviously to prudently provide for such extensions and additional accommodations as in a rapidly growing country like this, the public service will probably require at no distant day. The said act contains a provision appropriating the sum of $10,000,000 to be expended for the object contemplated in the act.

Another bill introduced on February 11, 1890, by Mr. Moody, in the Senate, provides that when any city, town, or village having 4,000 or more inhabitants, shall by its official act petition the Postmaster-General so to do, it shall be his duty, if the facts in the petition be found true, and if the petition be accompanied by a warranty deed for the site, to cause a suitable post-office building to be erected in such city, town, or village, the cost of which shall not be less than $10,000 nor more than $50,000. A provision of this act appropriates $3,000,000 for the purpose.

I think the Government need never be at a loss for some suitable and safe repository for such trust funds as it would receive in its savings banks. No such assumed or anticipated obstacle should for a moment be permitted to stand in the way of their establishment. We have the experience of nearly the whole civilized world to teach us their utility and beneficial influences, and the Congress which will bestow their privileges upon all the people will mark a memorable milestone in the history of our progress.

Yours, very truly,

JOHN WANAMAKER,
Postmaster-General.

Hon. JOHN H. MITCHELL,
United States Senate.

APPENDIX.

EXHIBIT 1.

H. R. 13404.

A BILL to establish postal savings banks and encourage small savings.

Be it enacted by the Senate and House of Representatives of the United States of America in Congress assembled, That the Postmaster-General is hereby authorized to direct such post-offices as he may designate as postal savings banks to receive deposits for remittance to the subdepositories as hereinafter provided for, and to repay the same to the depositors, or to their legal representatives, under such regulations as he may prescribe.

SEC. 2. That the Postmaster-General shall furnish and keep for sale at each postal savings bank adhesive stamps of the denominations of ten cents and one dollar, to be known as postal savings stamps, and shall also furnish and keep for use of the purchasers of said stamps postal savings cards, upon which such stamps when sold shall be affixed.

SEC. 3. That all postal savings moneys left with postmasters at the receiving offices, agreeably to the provisions of this act, shall be forwarded by them, at stated intervals to be fixed by the Postmaster-General, and not less frequently in any case than once a month, under regulations relating thereto, to such post offices of the first class as may be designated by the Postmaster-General as subdepositories of postal savings funds; and the postmasters at such subdepositories shall, at the end of every calendar month, make detailed reports to such officer of the Treasury as the Secretary of the Treasury may designate of all postal savings funds as shall have been received by them during the preceding month from the receiving offices, and at the same time furnish copies of said reports to the Postmaster-General ; and, also, transmit said moneys for deposit to such banks or banking institutions as may make application therefor to the Secretary of the Treasury, and be designated by him for the purpose, in such amounts, to be held at such rates of interest as the Secretary of the Treasury may provide for; and all such postal savings deposits are hereby declared to be preferred claims against the banks holding the same.

SEC. 4. That it shall be the duty of the Postmaster-General and Secretary of the Treasury to provide and issue interest-bearing certificates of deposit of the denominations of the twenty and one hundred dollars each, bearing interest at a rate not to exceed two and four-tenths of one per centum per annum upon deposits of twenty dollars or a multiple of twenty dollars; interest to be paid upon such deposits only as remain a period of not less than six months, and shall date from and begin the first of the calendar month following the deposit of the amount of twenty dollars or its multiple.

SEC. 5. That the Secretary of the Treasury is hereby authorized to loan to banks or approved depositories within the States, when such postal deposits are made, upon such securities and under such rules and regulations as he may prescribe, at a rate of interest not less than three per centum per annum, all such postal savings funds.

SEC. 6. That the amount of accumulations of deposits of any one individual shall not exceed five hundred dollars.

SEC. 7. That the banks receiving deposits of postal savings funds, as provided in this act, shall keep separate and distinct accounts of all receipts and payments, and a balance sheet of such accounts from the first of January to the thirty-first of December in every year, inclusive, and for any shorter period if the same be required, shall be filed with the Secretary of the Treasury and the Postmaster-General, and laid before Congress not later than the thirty-first day of January in every year.

SEC. 8. That it is hereby made the duty of the Postmaster-General and the Secretary of the Treasury to designate such officers and subdivisions of their respective Departments to take charge of all business in connection with postal savings funds as may be necessary.

19

SEC. 9. That the provisions of the several statutes relating to the larceny, embezzlement, or misappropriation of the postal funds, money-order funds, postage stamps, stamped envelopes, or postal cards, and to the forging or counterfeiting of postage stamps, the stamps printed upon stamped envelopes, or postal cards, or the dies, plates, or engraving used in the manufacture of the same, be and they are hereby extended, including the punishment prescribed therefor, and made applicable to the commission of similar crimes in connection with the postal savings system hereby established.

SEC. 10. That the Postmaster-General is hereby authorized and directed to promulgate rules and regulations, not inconsistent with law, for carrying out the purposes of this act, and for conducting the business to which relates.

Exhibit 2.

Interesting details of postal savings bank systems in Sweden, Great Britain, Austria, Belgium, The Netherlands, France, Russia, and Italy.

SWEDEN.

At the close of 1888 the number of post-offices empowered to transact savings-bank business was 1,841, as against 1,808 at the end of 1887. Although this increase is not as large as in the preceding year, still it corresponds to the increase in the number of post-offices, for in both years the percentage of post-offices acting as agencies of the post-office savings-bank in Sweden was 93. While in 1887 it became necessary to augment the number of post-office savings-banks in a larger measure in the two districts of Malmöhus and Kristianstad than in the rest of the country, the rate of increase in 1888 was about the same throughout the Swedish postal territory. The greatest number of newly established post-office savings banks in any one Government district was only 6 in the year under report, as against 18 in 1887. In the district of Göteborg och Bohus there was even a decrease in the number of savings-bank offices.

In comparing the number of post-office savings banks with the area and population of Sweden we find that there was, on an average, one such establishment to every 235,21 square kilometers and 2,597 inhabitants in 1888, while in 1884, the first year in which the institution was in operation, there was one postal savings-bank agency to as many as 274,93 square kilometers and 2,949 inhabitants. Although this does not constitute any considerable advance, yet it may be looked upon as satisfactory if the rather low rate of increase of the population in the country is taken into account.

The total amount of business done in 1888 showed a not inconsiderable increase. The deposits numbered 212,131 and aggregated 3,136,881 crowns, making, on an average, 45 deposits, amounting to 661 crowns, to every 1,000 inhabitants. In 1887 this average was but 40 as regards the number and 384 crowns as concerns the amount of deposits. The withdrawals did not show the same rate of increase; they reached the number of 41,287 and the total amount of 1,496,015 crowns, this being, on an average, 9 withdrawals, amounting to 315 crowns per 1,000 inhabitants.

A comparison of the business transacted by the post-office savings banks in 1888 and 1887 in the various government districts shows that in 1888 there was an increase in the number of deposits in all the districts with the exception of those of Södermanland, Blekinge, Kristianstad, Malhömus, Holland, Örebro, and Gefleborg, where the average number of deposits per 1,000 inhabitants was 51, 38, 17, 27, 29, 42, and 49 respectively, in 1888, as against 58, 39, 18, 30, 32, 43, and 57 in 1887. In the districts of Elfsborg and Vestmanland the deposits showed the same figures as in the preceding year.

There was an increase in the amount of deposits in all the districts, reaching in Kronoberg and Norbotten the unusually high percentage of 277 and 182. The number of withdrawals remained unchanged in 14 government districts. In the Stockholm City and 8 other districts it showed an increase, there being a falling off in 2 districts. The amount of withdrawals increased in all the districts except in that of Södermanland.

The growing interest of the public in the post-office savings bank is demonstrated by the increase in the number of depositors, which was 174,747 in 1888 as against 152,016 in 1887, the increase being 22,731, or 14.95 per cent. At the close of the year under review the amount on deposit reached 4,650,743.62 crowns, an increase of 1,765,346.87 crowns, or 61.18 per cent. over the preceding year. As compared with the population, the sum standing to the credit of depositors amounted on an average to 979.46 crowns per 1,000 inhabitants.

A comparison of the number of depositors and the amount on deposit in 1884 with the corresponding figures of the year under report shows that since the institution of the post-office savings bank in Sweden the number of depositors has increased by 95,234, or 119.77 per cent., and the total amount standing to their credit by 3,823,102.50 crowns, or 461.93 per cent.

There was a sensible decrease in the number of agencies for the sale of savings stamps as compared with the preceding year. One hundred and fifty-nine of these agencies held by private persons were closed. Although the administration took measures to meet the most urgent requirements by increasing the number of savings stamps agencies at post-offices by 41, there still remained an actual decrease of 118. The total number of agencies for the sale of savings stamps throughout the country was 4,224, there being thus 1 agency to 102.51 square kilometers, as against 1 to 99.73 square kilometers in 1887.

The number of savings stamps sold to the public was 801,028, and the value represented by them reached 80,102.80 crowns. A comparison of these figures with those of 1884 shows that in the course of the 5 years during which the post-office savings bank has been in existence the sale of savings stamps, which amounted to 1,558,676 in 1884, decreased to nearly one-half of its original figure.

According to the accounts of the post-office savings bank department for 1888 there was a considerable increase in the total amount of business transacted. In 1888 the receipts and payments reached the sum of 8,523,893.80 crowns as against 5,812,067.81 crowns in the preceding year, so that the financial results may be considered as entirely satisfactory. The cost of management only reached 1.59 per cent. of the total amount of transactions as compared with 2.33 per cent. in 1887.

The cost of management, both in itself and in proportion to the number of transactions effected in the course of the year, and the number of accounts open at the close of the year, was lower in Sweden than in the post-office savings banks of any of the other states.

GREAT BRITAIN.

(1890.)

There has been an increase in savings-bank business, though at a slightly lower rate than in 1888, when the amounts of the deposits transferred from trustee savings banks were unusually large.

The deposits in the year numbered 8,101,120, amounting to £19,814,308 as against 7,540,625 and £19,052,226, the number and amount for the year 1888. The withdrawals were 2,757,848 in number, amounting in all to £16,814,268, showing an increase of 124,040 in number and of £1,011,533 in amount over the number and amount for 1888. As a net result of these transactions a total sum of £62,999,620, including interest, remained to the credit of depositors on the 31st December, 1889, being an increase of £4,443,226 for the year as compared with an increase of £4,582,329 in 1888. The amount of interest credited to depositors was £1,443,186, or £110,348 more than in 1888.

The greatest number of deposits on one day was 55,095, amounting to £137,336, and made on the 30th December, but the largest amount deposited on one day was £158,-218 on the 31st December. The greatest number of withdrawals on one day was 18,499, amounting to £93,922, made on the 17th December. The average amount of each deposit was £2 2s. 11d. as compared with £2 10s. 6d. in 1888. This decrease is, however, chiefly due to the large amounts of many of the transfers from trustee savings banks in 1888. The average amount of each withdrawal was £6 1s. 11d. as compared with £6 in 1888.

The number of accounts opened in 1889 was 924,010, and 637,128 were closed. The corresponding numbers for 1888 were, respectively, 887,460 and 618,294. The total number of accounts opened at the end of the year was 4,507,809, or 286,882 more than in 1888, distributed as follows:

	Number.	Proportion to population.	Average balance due to each depositor.
			£ s. d.
England and Wales	4,162,529	1 to 7	13 19 5
Scotland	159,920	1 to 25	8 12 3
Ireland	185,360	1 to 25	18 14 11
United Kingdom	4,507,809	1 to 8	13 19 6

In 1888 the proportion to population and the average balance were, in England and Wales, 1 in 7 and £13 17s. 3d.; in Scotland, 1 in 27 and £8 8s. 11d.; and in Ireland, 1 in 28 and £18 15s. 4d., and in the United Kingdom 1 in 9 and £13 17s. 5d.

The total number of post-offices open for the transaction of savings-bank business on December 31, 1889, was 9,353, or 331 more than in 1888, of which 286 were opened in

England and Wales; 25 in Scotland, and 20 in Ireland. Whenever a new savings bank office is opened a handbill calling attention to the fact and describing the chief advantages of the post-office savings-bank system is distributed from house to house in the neighborhood.

The number of registered friendly societies authorized during the year to open accounts without limit as to amount in the post-office savings bank was 800, and the number of provident and charitable societies authorized to open accounts during the year was 2,197.

Only 284 penny banks invested their funds during 1889 as compared with 338 in 1888. Of the number last year 130 were connected with schools, of which 44 were board schools.

A novel experiment was made last year by the Ragged School Union as a first lesson in thrift. At the annual distribution of prizes 335 scholars received from the union deposit books showing that 5s. had been placed to the credit of each in the post-office savings bank. In ordinary circumstances the attendance of a depositor is required when an account is opened, but, as in this case, such a requirement would have made the arrangement impossible; all the necessary preliminaries were settled in coöperation with the secretary of the union, and the president, the Earl of Aberdeen, expressed publicly his thanks to the department for doing so. By a curious coincidence the same plan appears to have been adopted in Paris, where, at a party given in December last at the Elysée, to the pupils of the municipal schools, each child received, as well as toys and clothing, a savings bank book with an entry of a deposit of 10 francs.

Special arrangements also have been made to facilitate the deposit and withdrawal of money in other exceptional cases. On one occasion bonuses amounting to £1,680 were placed to the credit of 340 men employed in a large brewery. A post-office clerk attends regularly at Walmer Barracks on pay days to receive deposits, which, on an average, have numbered 66 at each visit. In the case of a regiment suddenly ordered on foreign service, arrangements were made for the repayment of deposits at 24 hours' notice.

The claims made by the representatives of deceased depositors numbered 20,740 as compared with 21,323 in 1888. The applications respecting the money of depositors who had become insane numbered 440 last year, and 377 in 1888. Under the new regulation made in that year 2,371 transfers of deposits from one account to another were made in 1889.

During the year 31 trustee savings banks were closed and deposits amounting to £716,814, and stock investments of the nominal value of £13,860, were transferred to the books of post-office savings bank, in addition to deposits amounting to £48,268, and £3,144 stock transferred in the ordinary course of business. In 1888 23 trustee savings banks were closed, but the total amount transferred was £1,133,497, with £22,389 stock.

AUSTRIA.

The Austrian post-office savings bank department has been able to publish a most satisfactory report on the business of this bank during the year 1889, which has developed in a highly successful manner. The aggregate results of the savings bank and check business considerably exceeded those of the preceding year. The savings bank transactions showed all desirable steadiness. Numerous persons belonging to the poorer classes joined the ranks of the depositors. The percentage of increase in the amount on deposit was higher than in any preceding year. The facilities for effecting check business were likewise extensively used by the public at large during the year under report. This fact is especially demonstrated by the great increase in the number of persons possessing check books, and by the considerable augmentation in the receipts and payments in this branch of the service.

In 1889 the aggregate amount of receipts and payments on check accounts exceeded 1¼ milliards of florins ; nearly one-half of these transactions were made at the Post-Office Savings Bank Department itself. A further satisfactory feature in the post-office savings bank business consists in the development of the clearing house transactions, the amount of which reached, as early as December, 1889, 29.2 per cent. of the total amount of the business done in all the branches of the post-office savings bank service. The gratifying results of the year 1889, which show an increase of 25 per cent. over the previous year, are the natural consequence of the satisfactory progress of business in all the departments.

We give below some particulars showing the details of the transactions effected :
In 1889 the savings bank deposits amounted, inclusive of interest, to 18,625,680 florins, and the withdrawals to 15,715,911, leaving an excess of deposits of 2,909,769 florins.

The number of savings bank accounts opened in 1889 was 131,071 ; in 1888, 121,729, being an increase over 1888 of 9,342.

The total number of savings bank accounts remaining open at the close of 1889 was 719,431, and at the end of 1888, 655,335, this being 64,096 accounts more than in 1888.

This is the highest increase which has taken place during 5 years, it having only been exceeded in the year next following that in which the post-office savings-bank system was started.

As a depositor is prohibited by the legal provisions to open more than one account for himself, the number of accounts open at the close of the year, also represents the number of depositors. In the course of 1889, 150 cases were discovered of persons having opened several accounts in their own favor. In accordance with the provisions in force the balances of the several accounts were added together by the post-office department and placed to the credit of a single account.

The greater part of the above-mentioned 719,431 depositors in the post-office savings bank, viz, 222,511, fall to the share of Lower Austria. Then follow Bohemia with 179,713 depositors, Moravia with 77,015, and Galicia with 68,674, the list being closed with the provinces of Styria, Tyrol, and Vorarlberg, Upper Austria, the Coast Lands (Görz, Gradisca, Istria, and Trieste), Silesia, Bukowina, Carniola, Salzburg, and lastly Dalmatia, where the number of depositors in the post-office savings bank is the smallest.

In the Austrian half of the monarchy, 31 in every 1,000 inhabitants were depositors in 1889; in 1888, the number of depositors compared with the population was only 29 to 1,000.

If we contrast the number of depositors in the post-office savings bank with the population of the various provinces, the order runs entirely differently from the above. Although we find Lower Austria still at the head of the list, and this with 88 depositors in 1,000 inhabitants, the order of the other provinces is completely changed, viz, Salzburg with 43, Silesia with 36, Moravia with 34, Upper Austria with 32, densely populated Bohemia with 31, Tyrol and Vorarlberg with 31, Carinthia with 30, Styria with 27, the Coast Lands (Istria, Görz, Gradisca, and Trieste) with 27, Bukowina with 19, Carniola with 17, Galacia with 11, and Dalmatia with 10 depositors in every 1,000 inhabitants.

The great majority of depositors, viz, nearly 76 per cent. belong to the German-speaking population of the monarchy. The rest is divided as follows among the various nationalities: 15 per cent. are Bohemians, 5 per cent. are Poles, 2.6 per cent. Italians, and a very small percentage are Slavonians, Croatians, Ruthenians, and Roumanians.

61.5 per cent. of all the depositors were men, 37.6 per cent. women, and 0.9 per cent were associations, corporations, etc.

84 per cent. of the depositors were able to write, and 14.4 per cent. were unable to do so; with regard to 0.6 per cent. of the depositors nothing was ascertained in this respect. The remainder was composed of associations, corporations, etc.

The statistical records taken with a view to a classification of the depositors according to their occupation or profession, afford a satisfactory proof of the fact that youthful depositors (children, school children, and students) were the most numerous class, forming as they did 33.5 per cent. of the new depositors. The extensive use made by the young of the post-office savings bank must partly be attributed to the efforts made by teachers and postal officers to foster a thrifty spirit among them. This category of depositors is followed by tradespeople, mechanics, and male and female servants. The number of societies, public offices, corporations, and institutions availing themselves of the post-office savings-bank was likewise very considerable. At the close of the year 1889, the list of the post-office savings bank depositors contained 3,110 societies of every kind, foremost among which were fire brigades, associations for the sick, school societies, trade associations, workingmen's societies, sporting societies, clubs, choral societies, savings and lottery societies, charitable associations, benevolent and religious societies, etc. More than half the number of these societies were in Bohemia, Lower Austria, and Tyrol.

At the close of 1889, the number of corporations and institutions having made deposits in the post-office savings bank numbered 2,296. More than half of this number were church administrations, ecclesiastical corporations, parishes, and prebends. The remainder were municipalities, institutes for the poor, school boards, foundations, Government offices, military messes, uniform and band funds, military and police headquarters, libraries, hospitals, etc.

In Austria an arrangement is in force according to which deposits can be made through the medium of rural messengers whose duty it is to pay over the money intrusted to them by the inhabitants of the rural district to the post-offices by which they are employed. In consequence of the praiseworthy zeal and intelligence with which this service is carried out, this branch of the savings bank business showed most satisfactory results in many rural delivery districts. In the course of 1889, deposits were collected by rural messengers in rural delivery districts and remitted to the post-office savings bank in 22,949 cases, the total amount collected in this manner being 675,726 florins. The most satisfactory results in this branch of business were obtained in Lower Austria and Bohemia, whereas in Galicia, Carniola, and the coast lands no transaction was effected through the medium of rural messengers.

As compared with the year 1888, there was an increase of 2,847 in the number of deposits collected by rural letter carriers, and of 68,927 florins in the amount of the same.

Judging from the facts and the satisfactory results recorded in the above summary, it may be expected that the Austrian post-office savings bank will continue in the path of progress, and that by its agency a thrifty spirit will be promoted among the poorer classes of the population, and their economic situation thereby be improved.

BELGIUM.

We gather from the last report of the Belgian savings and pension bank, that, in the course of 1888, 125,937 accounts were opened and 73,873 closed. The number of accounts remaining open at the end of the year was 598,675, of which 593,979 were in the names of private persons and 4,696 in those of public institutions, as against 546,611 accounts open at the close of the preceding year, of which 542,057 belonged to private persons and 4,554 to public institutions. 1,193,880 deposits were made of the total amount of 119,525,676 francs, making an average of 100.01 francs per deposit, as compared with 112.03 francs in 1887. The number of withdrawals was 319,338, aggregating 106,169,928 francs in amount, this being an average of 332.42 francs per withdrawal as against 380.89 francs in 1887.

The amount of interest added to the principal on the 31st of December, 1888, was 6,927,306 francs (6,160,285 francs in 1887), and the sum (inclusive of interest) standing to the credit of depositors on that date was 260,224,436 francs, viz, 249,998,195 francs to the credit of private depositors, and 10,226,243 francs to that of public institutions. The average amount standing to the credit of each account was, therefore, 434.67 francs as against 438.96 in 1887. The number of deposits effected to the credit of accounts current by communes and public institutions at the Central Bank, at the branches of the National Bank, and with the collectors of taxes was 29,159 for a total amount of 22,920,103 francs (as against 30,794 deposits for 25,076,391 francs in 1887), and that of withdrawals 47,209 for a total amount of 23,443,151 francs (as compared with 45,653 withdrawals amounting to 23,360,890 francs in 1887). The interest added to the capital was 98,486 francs (as against 106,560 francs in 1887), and the total amount, inclusive of interest, standing to the credit of these accounts current reached 8,100,360 francs (8,524,922 francs in 1887).

Thus the total amount standing to the credit of both the ordinary accounts and the accounts current on the 31st of December, 1888, was 268,324,798 francs (248,466,306 francs in 1887). The average amount of deposits below 100 francs was 13.62 francs. The percentage of deposits amounting to 100 francs and less was 90 (89 in 1887), and that of deposits exceeding the amount of 100 francs was 10 (11 in 1887). The percentage of accounts having on the 31st of December a balance of less than 100 francs was 65 (66 in 1887), and that of accounts with a balance exceeding 100 francs was 35 (34 in 1887).

In the course of the year under review the following definitive investments were made: 18,379,384.30 francs in Government stock, treasury bonds, and bonds of the "Classe d'Annuités;" 6,173,182.53 francs in bonds of the "Crédit communal," and treasury bills; 5,288,268.88 francs in bonds of Belgian companies; 997,000 francs in bonds of mortgage on houses; 404,600 francs in bonds of mortgage on landed property; and 6,669 francs in the savings bank premises.

The provisional investments were as follows: 78,221,371.08 francs in bills on Belgium; 278,779,517.09 francs in foreign bills, and 14,901,350 francs in loans granted on the security of stocks. The average rate of discount of the national bank was 3.32 per cent., while that of the savings bank (on Belgian bills) varied from to 3 to 5¼ per cent. The revenue from the definitive investments amounted to 5,794,824.19 francs, and that from the provisional investments to 2,703,371.44 francs, making a total revenue of 8,498,195.63 francs. At the close of 1888 the value of the definitive investments was 175,790,363.45 francs, and that of the provisional investments 84,824,307.73 francs. Thus, the total value of investments was 260,614,671.18 francs. The interest allowed to depositors amounted to 7,260,838.03 francs, and the cost of management to 639,896.41 francs. The net revenue transferred to the reserve fund was 597,461.19 francs, bringing this fund up to the sum of 7,238,599.78 francs at the close of 1888, as against 6,641,138.59 francs on the 31st of December, 1887.

The investments in the form of loans granted on the security of stocks gave rise to 772 transactions of a total amount of 14,901,350 francs, as against 859 transactions of an aggregate sum of 14,841,300 francs in 1887. Thus, the average amount of each transaction amounted to 19,302 francs.

A classification of the deposits made in 1888, according to the amount of each of them, shows that out of every 100 deposits, there were 77 per cent. of amounts between 1 and 20 francs, 12.9 of amounts between 20 and 100 francs, 6.8 of amounts between 100 and 500 francs, 1.7 of amounts between 500 and 1,000 francs, 1.5 of amounts between 1,000 and 5,000 francs, and 0.1 per cent. of amounts beyond 5,000 francs. There were 45 deposit books in every 100, with balances between 1 and 20 francs, 20.3 with from 20 to 100 francs, 15.9 with from 100 to 500 francs, 6.4 with from 500 to 1,000 francs, 11.2 with from 1,000 to 5,000 francs, and 1.2 with balances exceeding 5,000 francs.

According to the statistics of the school savings banks, these institutions showed the following results on the 31st of December, 1888:

Out of the 7,447 primary schools (inclusive of infant schools, and the schools of primary instruction attached to educational institutions of other classes) there were 4,798 which took part in the savings bank business. The number of children possessing deposit books was 154,192, viz, 86,309 boys and 67,883 girls. In addition to these, 40,929 children, 21,867 of whom are boys and 19,057 girls, make deposits without as yet possessing depositors' books. There were, therefore, 2,649 schools in which no savings bank business was transacted. These schools numbered 696,726 children, viz, 337,608 boys and 359,118 girls.

The total amount standing to the credit of children of primary schools reached 3,576,226.29 francs on the 31st of December, 1888, of which sum 1,960,111.42 francs belonged to boys and 1,616,114.87 francs to girls.

On the same date the number of middle-class schools and of educational establishments for adults in which savings bank business is transacted was 258, that of depositors was 5,731, and the amount standing to their credit reached 158,175.90 francs.

In adding up the above figures, we find that on the 31st of December, 1888, there was a total number of 5,056 schools of all kinds, in which 200,847 pupils of both sexes had saved a total amount of 3,734,402.19 francs. We may add that 199,724 pupils invested their savings, amounting to 3,701,759.54 francs in the Caisse générale d'epargne et de retraite under the guaranty of the state, while the others, 1,123 in number, possessing a total sum of 32,642.65 francs, either paid in their savings to private savings banks or invested them in government stock. Of the former, 155,370 pupils, whose savings amounted to the sum of 2,711,753.93 francs effected their deposit through the medium of the post-office.

THE NETHERLANDS.

At the close of the year 1888 the number of open accounts was 201,763 (169,027 at the end of 1887), this being an increase of 32,736 accounts, or 19.3 per cent., over the preceding year. The average number of deposits made by each depositor was 2.2, this average being only exceeded in the provinces of North Holland, North Brabant, and Utrecht (2.5, 2.3, and 2.3 per cent., respectively). On the other hand, the provinces of Limburg and Drente continued to show the lowest average, viz, 1.8, and 1.6 per cent. As regards the proportion between depositors and inhabitants, the province of North Holland still headed the list with 64.4 depositors to every 1,000 inhabitants; then followed South Holland (45.6), Utrecht (44.8), Limburg (43.7), and North Brabant (42.1), the province of Groningen coming last with 11.4 depositors per 1,000 inhabitants. The average throughout the country amounted to 41.5 per thousand.

In 1888 the average share of every 1,000 inhabitants in the total amount deposited throughout the Kingdom was 2,169.76 florins, as against 1,786.57 florins in 1887, and the average amount of each deposit 20.82.5 florins, as compared with 19.39 in the preceding year.

The number of deposits was 445,799 and the total amount 9,282,802.89 florins, this being an increase of 51,562 in the number and of 1,639,371.04 florins in the amount of deposits as compared with 1887.

There was an increase of 0.4 per cent. in the number of deposits effected by means of postage stamps, and a decrease of 1.3 per cent. in the number of deposits below 10 florins, as against 1887.

In 1888 the amount of withdrawals reached 29.1 per cent. of the total amount deposited in the course of the year added to the sum on deposit on the 31st of December, 1887, the number of withdrawals being 131,969 and their amount 6,773,168.93 florins. The average amount of each withdrawal was 51.32 florins (as against 51.42 florins in 1887).

The interest accruing from the invested deposits was 428,801.73 florins, while the interest allowed to depositors amounted to 318,051.67 florins, thus leaving for the year 1888 a surplus of 110,750.06 florins, which exceeded that obtained in 1887 by 14,553.52 florins. The average rate of interest yielded by the invested funds was 3.35 per cent.

The cost of management amounted to about 100,229.54 florins, this being 0.71 per cent. of the total amount due to depositors. In 1887 this item reached 0.84 per cent. of the amount on deposit.

In the course of 1888, the savings bank service was extended to 21 post-offices, while 4 auxiliary offices were closed for this branch of business. At the close of the year, 234 post-offices and 949 auxiliary offices, making a total of 1,183 establishments (1,164 in 1887), were open for the transaction of savings-bank business. At 38 or 3.2 per cent. (44, or 3.8 per cent. in 1887) of these establishments no transaction was effected.

42,719 of the 201,763 accounts open on the 31st of December, 1888, had a balance of less than 1 florin, 56,498 one of from 1 to 10 florins, 66,174 one of from 10 to 100 florins, and 36,372 one of 100 florins and more.

The annual percentage of increase in the number of accounts and in the amount due to depositors from 1882 to 1888, was as follows:

Year.	Number of accounts.	Amount on deposit.
	Per cent.	*Per cent.*
1882	102.5	135.0
1883	46.8	59.0
1884	33.6	44.5
1885	23.6	36.9
1886	24.6	39.2
1887	20.7	25.8
1888	19.4	20.5

There was an increase in the number of applications of withdrawal and of authorizations of repayment issued by the central direction transmitted by telegraph. In 1888 there were 55 telegraphic authorizations for the repayment of a total sum of 18,037.25 florins.

FRANCE.

We extract the following particulars from the report of the French ministry of commerce, industries, and the colonies, on the business of the French national savings bank for 1888:

In the course of 1888 the deposits reached 1,456,332 in number, and 169,348,619.19 francs id amount; on the other hand, the number of withdrawals was 536,891, aggregating 133,291,211.15 francs in amount. Thus, the deposits exceeded the withdrawals by 36,057,408.04 francs.

At the close of 1887, the amount standing to the credit of depositors was 223,519,-666.19 francs. If we add to this sum the above-mentioned excess of receipts over payments of 36,057,408.04 francs, and the interest added to the capital of depositors, in 1888, viz, 7,211,528.53 francs, we find that the total amount due to depositors at the close of 1888 was 266,788,602.76 francs.

The deposits are divided into two classes, namely, first deposits and subsequent deposits.

First deposits.

Year.	Number.	Amount.	Average amount per deposit.
		Francs.	*Francs.*
1882	227,438	47,606,879.75	210
1883	207,827	40,440,833.07	194
1884	222,159	46,780,639.82	210
1885	221,107	52,185,749.17	236
1886	239,502	58,522,168.38	244
1887	236,888	58,640,041.71	247
1888	261,966	67,573,159.67	257
	1,616,887	371,749,471.57	229

As this table shows, there was a considerable increase in the number and amount of first deposits. The average amount of each first deposit rose from 247 francs in 1887 to 257 francs in 1888.

The number of cases in which opposition was made in the course of 1888 was only 18 in more than 270,000 accounts opened by married women without the assistance of their husbands, and 2 in more than 540,000 accounts of minors opened without the assistance of their legal representatives. This is an additional proof of the expediency of the liberal provisions of the law of the 9th of April, 1881. Lastly, there were but 31 ordinary cases of opposition on the part of third persons in more than 1,000,000 accounts.

Of the 261,811 accounts opened in the course of the year, 150,253 are in the names of men, and 111,558 in those of women. In these totals the percentage of accounts opened to heads of agricultural, industrial, and commercial establishments was 7.03, to agricultural laborers 5.81, to factory hands 15.13, to domestic servants 11.82, to soldiers and sailors 2.65, to clerks 8.76, to artists 4.97, to proprietors, and ladies and gentlemen of private means, 14.94, and to minors having no calling 28.89.

Further, 155 accounts were opened for various associations, viz, 95 for societies of mutual assistance, 48 for assimilated societies, and 12 for other associations. The total number of accounts opened by societies of this kind from the 1st of January, 1882, to the 31st of December, 1888, was 844.

A statement of the subsequent deposits effected since the beginning of 1882 is given below:

Year.	Number.	Amount.	Average amount of each deposit.
		Francs.	*Francs.*
1882	245,717	17,027,502.06	09.29
1883	489,606	32,594,938.13	66.57
1884	694,972	47,316,475.00	68.80
1885	818,600	60,742,740.78	75.07
1886	956,846	74,710,132.09	78.07
1887	1,054,164	85,746,736.27	81.28
1888	1,193,814	101,739,643.87	85.22
	5,454,519	419,878,168.20	76.97

Thus, there was an increase of 13.16 per cent. in the number, and of 18.65 per cent. in the amount of subsequent deposits.

The average amount of each subsequent deposit, which was 81.28 francs in 1887, rose to 85.22 francs in 1888.

As compared with 1882 there was an increase of 385.84 per cent. in the number, and of 497.51 per cent. in the amount of subsequent deposits.

We complete these particulars with a tabulated statement of the deposits of all kinds (first and subsequent deposits) paid in since the beginning of 1882.

Year.	Number.	Amount.	Average amount of each deposit.
		Francs.	*Francs.*
1882	473,155	64,634,381.81	136.00
1883	697,433	73,035,771.20	104.72
1884	917,131	94,097,114.82	102.59
1885	1,039,707	112,928,489.95	108.61
1886	1,196,348	133,232,300.47	111.36
1887	1,291,852	144,386,777.98	111.76
1888	1,455,780	169,312,803.54	116.30
	7,071,406	791,627,639.77	111.94

Thus there was an increase of 12.68 per cent. in the number and of 17.26 per cent. in the amount of deposits, as compared with 1887, and one of as much as 207 per cent. in the number and of 161 per cent. in the amount of these transactions as against 1882.

The above figures comprise both the deposits effected by means of savings-stamps and the amounts transferred from private savings banks to the national savings bank. From the beginning of 1882 to the close of 1888 these transfers were 68,368 in number and 13,064,023.83 francs in amount, the average amount of each transfer being thus 191.08 francs. There is a steady decrease both in the number and in the amount of the transfers effected from private savings banks to the national savings bank; an increase is only observable in the average amount of each transfer, which rose from 148 francs in 1882 to 277 francs in 1888. On the other hand, 16 accounts, with an aggregate amount of 9,299.60 francs, were transferred from the national savings bank to private savings banks.

The repayments are divided into two classes: (1) Partial and total repayments, and (2) investments in Government stock on behalf of depositors.

Partial and total repayments.

Year.	Number.	Amount.	Average amount of each repayment.
		Francs.	*Francs.*
1852	52, 540	16, 410, 817. 90	312. 34
1883	145, 934	42, 154, 983. 65	288. 26
1884	213, 230	56, 025, 991. 86	262. 74
1885	288, 784	74, 752, 309. 38	258. 15
1886	377, 613	97, 848, 996. 34	259. 12
1887	454, 855	112, 904, 198. 81	248. 22
1888	533, 372	129, 200, 313. 17	242. 23
	2, 066, 328	529, 297, 611. 11	256. 15

The rate of increase in the partial and total repayments which, in 1887, was 20.45 per cent. as regards the number, and 15.38 per cent. as concerns the amount of the same as compared with 1886, decreased to 17.26 and 14.43 per cent., respectively, in 1888. The average amount of each repayment, which was 248.22 francs in 1887, decreased to 242.23 francs in 1888.

From the beginning of 1882 to the close of 1888 there was an increase of 915.17 per cent. in the number, and of 687.28 per cent. in the amount of these repayments.

In 1888 the transactions of all kinds (deposits and withdrawals) were 1,992,445 in number and 302,528,016.31 francs in amount, this being an increase over 1887 of 241,860, or 13.81 per cent., as regards the number, and of 40,637,270.57 francs, or 15.51 per cent. as concerns the amount of these transactions.

The average number of transactions effected at each post-office, which was 87 in 1882, gradually rose to 136 in 1883, 174 in 1884, 201 in 1885, 237 in 1886, 260 in 1887, and 294 in 1888.

The number of post-offices entrusted with the transaction of savings bank business increased from 6,024 in 1882, to 6,193 in 1883, 6,478 in 1884, 6,620 in 1885, 6,649 in 1886, 6,712 in 1887, and 6,765 in 1888.

The amount of interest credited to depositors in 1888 was 7,211,528.53 francs, as against 5,988,768.01 francs in 1887.

RUSSIA.

The establishment of postal and telegraph savings banks in Russia was sanctioned by an imperial decree of the 26th of July (7th of August), 1889. These banks will carry on business in coöperation with the existing savings banks of the imperial bank under regulations, the principal of which are given below.

The management of the savings banks of the imperial bank shall, with the approval of the manager of the imperial bank, be intrusted to the postal administration at any place where the chief postal and telegraph administration shall consider this measure as necessary.

The minister of the interior is, with the approval of the minister of finances and of the imperial comptroller, empowered to issue regulations for the management of the postal and telegraph savings banks, and, if necessary, to fix the amount of the funds to be placed at the disposal of these banks.

In order to control the amount of deposits, the minister of the interior may, with the approval of the minister of finances, issue savings stamps, the designs of which shall be submitted to the managing senate for publication.

The minimum amount of a deposit is fixed at 25 kopeks, and the maximum amount standing to the credit of any depositor at 1,000 roubles.

The deposits paid in to the postal and telegraph savings banks shall enjoy all the privileges granted with regard to the deposits in the savings banks of the imperial bank.

The commission paid to postal and telegraph officers for the management of the savings banks shall be defrayed out of the total profit of the savings banks of the imperial bank. This commission amounts to 10 kopeks for each new deposit book issued, 10 kopeks for each amount of 100 roubles deposited, and 10 kopeks at the close of the year for every account that has been open for not less than 1 year. The amount of commission paid to each postal and telegraph savings bank may not be less than 50 roubles per annum.

The commission paid to the employés of the savings banks of the imperial bank, shall be defrayed out of the total profits of the savings banks of this bank. It shall not exceed one-half of the amounts fixed for the officers of the postal and telegraph savings banks.

The deposit books and all other forms are exempt from stamp duty.

The correspondence exchanged between the postal and telegraph savings banks, as well as with the savings banks of the imperial bank, is forwarded free of postage.

ITALY.

In 1887, for the first time since they were inaugurated, the Italian post-office savings banks record a decrease in the deposits as compared with the preceding year. While the deposits made in 1886 exceeded those paid in during 1885 by nearly 21,000,000 lire, the savings banks received 4,000,000 lire less in 1887 than in 1886.

The excess of deposits over withdrawals only reached 13,000,000 lire, which is the least satisfactory result obtained since the year 1878.

This regrettable state of things is to be ascribed, in the first place, to the economical crisis through which the country is passing. In the second place, it may be attributed to the reduction of rate of interest paid by the post-office saving's bank from 3½ to 3¼ per cent., which took place in 1887, and lastly, to the rumor prevailing in different provinces of the Kingdom that the Government intended temporarily to forbid the repayment of deposits. There is no doubt that this calumny was spread for the purpose of diverting payment of savings from the post-office to some local private savings bank. It is further possible that certain unsound political theories were at the root of the matter. The administration of the post-office savings bank did not think it expedient officially to contradict the false rumor. The only measure it took with a view to putting a stop to it consisted in an order to its offices not to put the slightest difficulty in the way of applications for the withdrawal of deposits, but on the contrary to effect repayments, whenever possible, on demand. In spite of adverse circumstances the affluence of the public to the post-office saving's banks was as considerable in 1887 as in previous years while the amount of business transacted was large, as may be seen by the following figures:

In 1887 the number of post-offices having transacted savings-bank business was 4,237; that of deposits, 1,920,545; of withdrawals, 1,069,193; of accounts opened, 288,925; of accounts closed, 109,428. The number of accounts opened thus exceeded that of accounts closed by 179,497. The amount of deposits was 159,417,724 lire. The amount of withdrawals was 146,250,099 lire. The amount of interest added to the principal in the first and second five years' periods since the creation of the bank was 7,226,322 lire. The deposits, inclusive of interest, exceeded the withdrawals by 20,393,946 lire, and the total amount on deposit in the post-office savings-bank reached the sum of 240,235,163 lire.

With the exception of the above-mentioned decrease of 4,000,000 in the amount deposited, all these figures denote sound progress, and the administration of the institution has no doubt that, as soon as these momentary difficulties have been overcome, the business of the bank will again proceed as hitherto on the path of improvement.

In the course of 1887, 140 post-offices were opened for the transaction of savings-bank business, so that at the close of the year the total number of post-office savings-banks amounted to 4,237.

The Italian postal administration has succeeded in extending post-office savings-bank service till its sphere of business has become almost identical with that of the potals service, and henceforth the establishment of post-office savings banks will keep pace with the opening of new post-offices.

Out of the 4,237 post-offices in the kingdom empowered to transact savings bank business, 10 effected no transaction, 14 effected only repayments, 352 received less than 1,000 lire, 947 received between 1,000 and 5,000 lire, 686 received between 5,000 and 10,000 lire, 1,539 received between 10,000 and 50,000 lire, 398 received between 50,000 and 100,000 lire, 291 received 100,000 lire and more.

The most important fact resulting from these figures is that there was a further decrease in the number of post-offices at which no transactions were made.

While in 1877 the number of post-offices open to the public for the deposit and withdrawal of savings, which did no business of this kind, was 848, this number decreased, notwithstanding the constant increase in the number of post-office savings banks to 594 in 1878, 282 in 1879, 141 in 1880, 94 in 1881, 53 in 1882, 41 in 1883, 29 in 1884, 21 in 1885, 18 in 1886, 10 in 1887, which is a proof that owing to the extension of the service to small localities at a great distance from the large centers of traffic, its advantages are more valued every day.

Satisfactory results were obtained by the savings banks in the schools of Italy, 5,401 teachers having undertaken the collection of savings. The sum deposited in this manner by 87,764 pupils reached 464,697 lire, and was paid in by the teachers to the post-office savings bank. Deposits were made by one-third of the pupils of those educational establishments in which so-called school savings banks exist. As compared with the preceding year, all these figures show a considerable increase, which permits of the conclusion that the teachers recognize more and more the utility of the school savings bank which—if well managéd and kept within proper limits—must certainly be considered as a powerful means of education.

From a general point of view, the position of the Italian post-office savings bank may be summed up as follows : This beneficent institution, in spite of the difficult conditions with which it has to contend, extends its sphere of business from year to year, gains more friends every year, and is a powerful means of promoting the prosperity of the Italian people in general, and of the working classes in particular.

EXHIBIT 3.

OPINIONS OF PREVIOUS POSTMASTERS-GENERAL.

HON. J. A. J. CRESWELL—1871.

The Post-Office Department is now prepared to undertake the organization and management of the telegraph in connection with its other duties. Indeed, I believe that the Department itself can aid materially in raising the money needed for the purchase through post-office savings banks, if Congress will authorize their establishment. The security of the Government being the best that could be obtained, many depositors would give it the preference over every other. By paying 4 per cent. interest, at the most, on deposits, a large fund could be readily accumulated and invested, under the direction of the Treasury Department, in the public securities. The proceeds of these investments could be used to reimburse the original purchase-money and all other expenditures for construction and repairs.

To prove the feasibility of this plan, I recur to the history of the British office. Savings banks in connection with post-offices were established in Great Britain on the 16th of September, 1861, with a limitation in the law creating them that they should not pay exceeding 2¼ per cent. interest on deposits. The following table will show with what rapidity and to what extent they have been intrusted with the money of the people:

Period.	Number of post-office savings banks.	Number of deposits.	Amount of deposits.	Total sum standing to credit of post office savings banks on books of national debt commissioners at close of the year.	Balance in hands of post-master-general, after allowing for charges of management, at close of the year.	Total balance in hand applicable to payment of depositors at close of the year.
From Sept. 16, 1861, to Dec. 31, 1862....	2,535	639,216	£2,114,660	£1,659,032	£35,602	£1,604,724
Year 1863............	2,991	842,848	2,651,209	3,328,182	44,413	3,372,595
1864............	3,081	1,110,762	3,350,000	4,995,663	5,522	5,001,185
1865............	3,321	1,302,309	3,719,017	6,582,329	4,327	6,586,656
1866............	3,507	1,525,871	4,400,657	8,231,176	25,791	8,256,967
1867............	3,629	1,502,344	4,643,906	9,867,703	47,690	9,915,393
1868............	3,813	1,757,303	5,333,638	11,963,053	Nil.	11,899,400
1869............	4,047	1,998,644	5,787,218	13,755,547	19,386	13,774,933
1870............	4,082	2,135,993	6,995,121	15,305,040	158,888	15,463,928

The total amount in hand after 10 years' operations, and for which the British Government pays only 2¼ per cent. interest, is £15,463,928, or $75,145,690—a much larger sum than will be required for the purchase and thorough repair of all the telegraphic lines in the United States.

Convinced of the wisdom of establishing the postal telegraph and post-office savings banks in this country, I earnestly recommend the passage by Congress of the laws necessary therefor.

HON. J. A. J. CRESWELL.—1872.

Post-office savings banks have been in operation in the United Kingdom since the 16th of September, 1861, and have steadily grown in popular confidence and favor. During the year 1871 the number of depositors increased 120,000, and the amount of deposits nearly £2,000,000. The total number of depositors is now 2,362,621, and the total sum standing to the credit of the post-office £17,303,815, or about $84,000,000. These figures show conclusively the utility of postal savings banks; and I renew my recommendation of last year for their establishment in this country.

HON. J. A. J. CRESWELL—1873.

The events of the past few weeks have awakened a lively interest in a plan heretofore submitted for securing the savings of the great body of the people by a pledge of the credit and faith of the United States. In my reports for 1871 and 1872 I urged the organization of institutions for that purpose, under the title of "Post-Office Savings Banks." The name was not well chosen. The institutions I have in view and recommend are not designed, and should not be permitted, to encroach upon the legitimate powers and duties of the national banks. They are totally distinct from the banks in their scope and character, in the machinery they employ, and in the ends they are intended to accomplish, and may be more accurately designated as postal savings depositories of the United States.

The financial difficulties in which the country has been unexpectedly involved, and which still continue to oppress it, have demonstrated the necessity for some means of maintaining confidence in times of threatened disaster, and of gathering and wisely employing the immense wealth scattered among the people, to prevent panic and escape the ruin which inevitably follows in its track. That the people of the United States hold the reins of financial as well as political power clearly appears from the following tables taken from the public debt statements, reports of the national banks and from official accounts:

Treasury notes of all kinds, including fractional currency, in the Treasury, in the national banks, and in the hands of the public on June 30, 1869, 1870, 1871, 1872, and 1873.

Date.	Aggregate.	In the Treasury.	In national banks.	In the hands of the public.
June 30, 1869	$388,118,859.73	$37,097,818.89	$82,738,974.53	$268,282,066.31
June 30, 1870	395,984,940.48	28,045,067.19	90,758,465.39	270,281,407.90
June 30, 1871	396,679,380.06	9,533,363.15	124,298,373.22	262,847,643.69
June 30, 1872	398,444,131.52	15,321,689.87	125,063,881.12	258,058,560.53
June 30, 1873	432,609,332.94	*41,513,529.77	108,204,050.84	282,891,752.33

*Thirty-one million seven hundred and thirty thousand dollars of the currency in the Treasury June 30, 1873, represents special deposits for redemption of certificates of deposit issued under act of June 8, 1872, which certificates are held by the national banks as part of their reserve of lawful money.

National bank notes held by the banks and the public on June 30, 1869, 1870, 1871, 1872, and 1873.

Date.	Aggregate.	On hand.	In the hands of the public.
June 30, 1869	$299,742,474.95	$17,915,295.95	$281,827,179.00
June 30, 1870	299,267,486.35	23,056,596.35	276,210,890.00
June 30, 1871	317,616,919.20	26,101,252.20	291,515,667.00
June 30, 1872	337,240,692.30	23,162,340.30	314,078,352.00
June 30, 1873	346,777,827.30	26,432,588.30	320,345,239.00

Recapitulation of currency in the hands of the public.

Date.	Treasury issues.	National bank notes.	Total.
June, 1869	$268,282,066.31	$281,827,179.00	$550,109,245.31
June, 1870	270,281,407.90	276,210,890.00	546,492,297.90
June, 1871	262,847,643.69	291,515,667.00	554,363,310.69
June, 1872	258,058,560.53	314,078,352.00	572,136,912.53
June, 1873	282,891,752.33	320,345,239.00	603,236,991.33
Aggregate for 5 years			2,826,338,757.76
Average			565,267,731.55

On the 30th of June last the public held, independent of the Treasury and the banks, $603,236,991.33. The amount of currency was then considered sufficient for all business purposes. In the month of August following, a stringency began to be felt in the money market, and we have since witnessed the extraordinary spectacle of the banks suspending and declaring their inability to pay United States notes or bank notes, or even fractional currency, to their depositors. Of course, under such circumstances, they could not continue to make their usual discounts for the accommodation of their customers. This can only be accounted for upon the theory of a general lack of confidence on the part of the people, and a consequent refusal to deposit, or invest, or even pay out in discharge of obligations the currency held by them. To meet this strange state of affairs, and to prevent a recurrence of the like in the future, many plans have been suggested—one involving an expansion of the currency, another compelling a return to specie payment, and still another providing for the issue by the Government of a convertible bond at a low rate of interest—but all open to objections more or less serious. The opinion is universal that if there could be a general restoration of confidence there would immediately be let loose an ample circulation for the entire country. If, therefore, a plan can be devised that will afford to depositors equal security to that afforded to note-holders, but little doubt can be entertained that a general amelioration of the present condition will be effected. The immense sum of $600,000,000 held by the people in June last, with the large accessions since made thereto by heavy drafts upon the Treasury and the banks, will be brought out from its place of concealment and applied to its legitimate work of aiding in forwarding our crops and products to market and in sustaining our vast manufacturing and other business interests.

In my judgment, a system of postal savings depositories would powerfully contribute to this most desirable consummation. Throughout the plan for their organization and work two ideas predominate : first, the United States is to insure the safe return of principal and interest whenever demanded ; and, secondly, the extensive machinery of the Post-Office is to be used to bring its advantages home to the great mass of the people. The details would be simple, safe, and efficient. Money-order offices, as agents of the Government, would receive deposits in small sums, ranging from one dollar upward to the limit fixed by law, which sums the postmaster would forward at short intervals to the nearest depository of the United States Treasury. A certificate, fixing the responsibility of the Government, would be issued immediately to the depositor by the postmaster, and notice thereof would be sent either to the Department or some established branch office, to the end that due entry thereof might be made and a more formal acknowledgment forwarded to the depositor. No depositor should be allowed in any one year to deposit exceeding $300 ; no greater accumulation of deposits should be permitted for any one depositor than $1,000 ; and no greater accumulation of deposits and interest should be allowed than $1,500.

Meantime, however, the United States should contract to pay interest not exceeding 4 per cent., to be computed from the first day of the month following the deposit, and to stop upon the first day of the month in which any withdrawal might be made. Interest should be computed to the end of the fiscal year, and then, if not drawn, should be added to the principal. It would of course be necessary to keep an exact account of all such deposits, and of the expenses incident to the management thereof, in the Treasury Department ; also to make provision for the payment of the amounts due depositors whenever and wherever they might desire to withdraw them ; and to allow and credit to such accumulations a somewhat greater rate of interest than that paid depositors, so that all expenses might be paid out of the fund and the institution made self-sustaining. I am confident that the plan of operations thus generally sketched may be so amplified and guarded that the people could be efficiently served, and the Government saved from all loss or expense.

The great ends to be attained are, first, absolute security ; secondly, the utmost facilities for deposits, withdrawals, and transfers ; and thirdly, perfect secrecy. A system thus organized and conducted would not only encourage economy and habits of saving on the part of all who might be in the way of earning small sums of money, but would tend largely to utilize and keep in circulation the immense amounts which are paid out for wages and in business, and give every depositor a direct interest in the stability of the Government. It would strengthen our national finances by pouring these accumulations into the Treasury, which, in turn, by judicious investments, could afford to monetary and banking institutions the very relief they now so eagerly seek. Thousands who doubt the security of the banks and savings institutions, whether private or organized under State laws, would cheerfully place their surplus money upon such terms in the keeping of the Government.

The extent of the benefits which will inure to the people and the Government from the establishment of this system will be best indicated by a statement of the amounts deposited in existing savings banks in some of the States of the Union. With the means of information at my command, I am able to make only a partial statement under this head. Congress wisely provided by the act of February 19, 1873, for an annual report to be made by the Comptroller of the Currency of the condition of all banks, banking companies, and savings banks organized under the laws of the several States and Territories ; but, on application to that officer, I have been informed that he has not yet succeeded in collecting the information necessary for such a report, and that in many of the States and Territories no returns are made by the savings banks, either to the legislature or any State officer, and that thus they are left without any supervision whatever. I regret that I shall be deprived for the present of the experience and industry which will doubtless be applied to the discharge of the duty imposed by the law referred to.

In the table following, the returns for Massachusetts are brought up to the 26th of October, 1862; for Rhode Island, Maine, and New Hampshire, to the year 1869-'70; for Connecticut, to January 1, 1871; for the State of New York, to January 1, 1873; and for California, to July 1, 1872:

State.	No. of savings institutions.	Number of depositors.	Amount deposited.	Average to each depositor.
Massachusetts	172	630, 246	$184, 797, 313. 92	$293. 21
Rhode Island	25	67, 238	27, 067, 072. 00	402. 55
Maine	36	39, 527	10, 490, 368. 00	265. 40
New Hampshire	45	71, 536	18, 759, 461. 00	262. 25
Connecticut		178, 000	55, 000, 000. 00	310. 00
New York	150	822, 642	285, 286, 621. 00	346. 79
California		58, 713	47, 784, 372. 00	
		1, 867, 802	629, 185, 207. 92	

Thus seven States had, many months ago, 1,867,802 depositors, and $629,185,207.92 on deposit, an amount greater by $3,476,930 than all the deposits, including those of individuals, the United States, and United States disbursing officers, held by all the national banks of the United States, numbering 1,919, on the 3d day of October, 1872.

Objection has been made to the establishment of postal savings depositories upon the ground that they would interfere with and overthrow the present savings banks. I respectfully submit that this objection is without foundation. Savings banks were originally established by the benevolent and philanthropic to provide safe places of deposit for the small savings of laboring people, and in the beginning they were conducted without hope of either profit or reward other than that which comes from the consciousness of doing good. In so far as they have since been used for purposes of speculation, their managers have diverted them from their original design, and to that extent have abused the confidence reposed in them. Security is to be sought above all other considerations, and hence the spirit of speculation should be thoroughly eradicated from their administration. If savings banks are subjected to risks and prostituted for purposes of gain for their managers, they should be overthrown. If, on the contrary, they continue to be well and profitably managed, and pay a greater rate of interest than that paid by the Government, they will in nowise be put to disadvantage, because every depositor will be left free to select his place of deposit.

Nor can the national banks raise a valid objection. They are organized to afford facilities to the community by lending money on personal security, dealing in exchange, issuing notes, and receiving deposits, not for permanent investment, but as temporary custodians. Bankers should own the capital they employ. When they attempt to do business on borrowed capital they are operating on a fictitious credit and become mere speculators. If they succeed in realizing more interest than they pay they make a profit by raising the price of money above its value. If they do not succeed in so doing, then, like other unfortunate speculators, they fail, and their creditors become their dupes. Hence a law prohibiting the payment of interest by the banks would simply confine them to their legitimate business, and prevent them from assuming improper risks. With the Government it is totally different. Its obligations must be met by resorting either to loans or taxation, and in determining its choice of alternatives, the paramount consideration should be the best interests of the people, whose agent it is. Sound policy dictates that the Government should lose no opportunity of borrowing from its own people, at a low rate of interest, for the purpose of discharging an indebtedness abroad, or relieving industry and enterprise at home from the trammels of taxation. But when the Government can arrest panic, restore confidence, call forth the hoarded treasure of the country, and revive the pursuits of industry, by a simple pledge of the people's credit for the people's security, who will say that that pledge should not be given?

Another objection is the tendency to centralization. To this I answer, that, if to establish postal savings depositories would be in violation of the Constitution, there is an end of the matter at once. If, on the contrary, such action would not be unconstitutional, then the only question is whether their establishment would on the whole be advantageous for the people and the Government. Since the national Government has assumed to organize and control the banking of the country, and has found warrant of law for undertaking the transmission of the people's money through the mails, it would appear that it is only discharging its whole duty and completing its financial work by providing for the safety of the small savings of the industrious and frugal poor. If, in addition, it can be shown that postal savings depositories will serve to fortify the national credit, make more equable the financial operations of the country, cultivate habits of thrift among the industrial classes, and illustrate the excellence of our institutions by protecting and augmenting the accumulations of self-denying toil, and thus in time merging the workman into the capitalist, the cry of centralization can not be made to drown the voice of the people in their demand that the Government of the United States shall execute for their benefit the high offices enjoined upon it by the Constitution.

Another objection, more practical, if not more tenable, is based on an alleged increase of expenses and public officers. So far as the establishment of savings-depositories would have any effect upon appointments, its tendency would be to secure a better class of officers in all respects. None but competent persons could discharge the duties of such institutions, and no man or party having a reputation to sustain would be willing to commit interests so important to unworthy hands. The Government would seek its principal agents and employés among experienced men wherever they could be found. A numerous force of additional officers would not be required. Many persons already employed in the postal service could be made to discharge a portion of the required duties. A force far less than that now needed in savings banks would be sufficient, with the assistance of the machinery of the post-office, to accomplish the same amount of work, and this, together with a supervising bureau in the Post-Office Department and the necessary accounting officers in the Treasury, is all that would be needed. The fact that the money-order office during the past year received transmitted, and paid out nearly $60,000,000, shows how well that branch of the Post-Office discharges its duties. I am entirely satisfied that the character of the service would be elevated, and the work more cheaply and better done by Government officers, controlled at every step by law, and punishable by severe penalties in case of default or embezzlement, than is possible under the present irresponsible and inefficient mode in which savings banks are conducted in many of the States.

But the argument by example is, perhaps, the most powerful. Let us, then, invoke the experience of other nations. The savings bank, like many other products of Christian civilization, was perfected piecemeal. An institution of a kindred character was founded at Hamburg as early as 1778, and first gave a demonstration of the power of small sums contributed by many when aggregated, though, it is stated, its operations were confined to the granting of deferred annuities. An institution approaching nearer to the savings bank, it is generally believed, was formed at Berne, Switzerland, in 1787. The idea, however, was fully developed in England, and the honor of its first practical application is divided among several persons, all of whom may claim to be benefactors of their race. In the year 1798 a friendly society for the benefit of women and children was established under the superintendence of Mrs. Priscilla Wakefield, and before the year 1801 there had been combined with its main design a twofold improvement, namely, a fund for loans and a bank for savings. In 1804 the savings bank was more regularly organized, and Mr. Eardley Wilmot, M. P., and Mr. Spurling were appointed trustees. A prior claim, however, is raised on behalf of Rev. Joseph Smith, of Wendover, who, in 1799, circulated in his parish proposals to receive deposits during the summer and return the amount at Christmas with an addition of one-third as a bounty.

The first publication in England of the idea of savings banks, under the name of frugality banks, is also attributed to the celebrated Jeremy Bentham as early as 1797. The society next formed was opened, in 1808, at Bath, chiefly through the instrumentality of certain ladies, who received deposits from female servants. In 1810 the first savings bank in Scotland was formed by Rev. Henry Duncan, minister of Ruthwell, Dumfriesshire, and in November, 1815, the providence institution of Southampton was established, under the patronage of the Right Honorable George Rose. The seeds thus sown rapidly germinated, took root, and soon exhibited a vigorous growth. By the year 1817 there had been formed no less than 70 banks in England, 4 in Wales, and 4 in Ireland by the voluntary association of benevolent persons. Parliament then took up the question, and by two separate acts recognized and organized banks for savings in England and Ireland, and two years later, in Scotland. Thenceforth such institutions were under the protection and guidance of the law, and much labor was expended in the effort to protect them from peculation and fraud; notwithstanding all which, it has been stated by competent authority, that between the years 1844 and 1857 frauds were perpetrated to the amount of £228,-800. The effect was disastrous in the extreme. Confidence was destroyed, and the disposition to economize became a subject of ridicule. Attention is called to the following:

Table showing the amount of deposits and withdrawals and the capital of savings banks, in the United Kingdom at the end of each year from 1841 to 1861, inclusive.

Year ended November 20—	Deposits.	Withdrawals.	Capital of savings banks in the United Kingdom.
1841	£5, 694, 908	£5, 487, 723	£24, 536, 971
1842	5, 789, 203	5, 656, 160	25, 400, 642
1843	6, 327, 125	5, 333, 015	27, 244, 266
1844	7, 160, 465	5, 710, 275	29, 653, 180
1845	7, 153, 176	6, 097, 042	30, 950, 983
1846	7, 300, 367	7, 255, 654	31, 851, 238
1847	6, 649, 008	9, 060, 075	30, 236, 032
1848	5, 862, 742	8, 653, 108	28, 114; 136
1849	6, 196, 883	6, 522, 760	28, 537, 010
1850	6, 363, 690	6, 760, 328	28, 930, 982
1851	6, 782, 059	6, 305, 500	30, 277, 654
1852	7, 281, 177	6, 684, 906	31, 754, 261
1853	7, 653, 520	7, 116, 330	33, 362, 260
1854	7, 400, 141	7, 950, 347	33, 736, 080
1855	7, 188, 211	7, 654, 133	34, 263, 135
1856	7, 741, 453	8, 023, 583	34, 946, 012
1857	7, 581, 415	8, 375, 095	34, 145, 567
1858	7, 901, 925	7, 839, 903	30, 220, 302
1859	9, 021, 907	7, 335, 349	38, 995, 876
1800	9, 478, 585	8, 258, 422	41, 258, 368
1861	8, 764, 870	9, 621, 539	41, 546, 475
Total	151, 298, 830	152, 313, 312	
Excess of withdrawals		1, 014, 482	

It is worthy of note that during the years 1847, 1848, 1849, and 1850 the withdrawals exceed the deposits by amounts respectively of £2,411,067, £2,790,366, £328,877, and £396,638, and that in the years 1854, 1855, 1856, 1857, and 1861, also, the withdrawals largely exceeded the deposits. The remarkable fact is also revealed that, taking the whole period between 1841 and 1861, when the increase in population in England and Wales was 4,190,496, when the exports increased from £51,545,116 to £125,102,814, and when the amount of wages paid must have been largely increased, the withdrawals actually exceeded the deposits by £1,014,482. The commercial crisis of 1847-'48, and the scarcity of money during the Crimean war, had, no doubt, a marked effect during some of the years recorded in the foregoing table; but the general result can be accounted for on no other theory than that the confidence of the masses had been weakened by the discovery of the enormous frauds above mentioned, the knowledge of the defects of the system, and the divided responsibility under which it was worked.

It thus became apparent that a radical reform must be effected, otherwise the usefulness of savings banks would be seriously impaired. After numerous failures a project for post-office savings banks was finally brought to the attention of Sir Rowland Hill, who gave it his cordial approval. A plan having been finally matured by Mr. George Chetwynd, and approved by Mr. Frank Ives Scudamore, fixing the rate of interest at 2½ per cent., it was carried through Parliament under the powerful championship of Mr. Gladstone, and became the law of the land on the 17th day of May, 1861. The details being approved, and the necessary machinery provided, it went into effect on the 17th day of September following. The annexed table, covering its operations from that date until the 31st day of December, 1872, proves its steady and uniform growth and its triumphant success.

Operations of the British post-office savings banks.

Period.	Number of post-office savings banks.	Number of deposits.	Amount of deposits.	Total sum standing to credit of post-office savings banks on books of national-debt commissioners at close of the year.	Balance in hands of post-master-general after allowing for charges of management at close of the year.	Total balance in hand applicable to payment of depositors at close of the year.
			£	£	£	£
From Sept. 16, 1861, to—						
Dec. 31, 1862.....	2,535	639,216	2,114,069	1,659,032	35,692	1,094,724
1863.....	2,991	842,848	2,651,209	3,328,182	44,413	3,372,595
1864.....	3,081	1,110,762	3,350,000	4,995,063	5,522	5,001,185
1865.....	3,321	1,302,309	3,719,017	6,582,329	4,327	6,586,656
1866.....	3,507	1,525,871	4,400,657	8,231,176	25,791	8,256,967
1867.....	3,629	1,592,344	4,643,906	9,867,703	47,690	9,915,393
1868.....	3,813	1,757,303	5,333,638	11,963,053	Nil.	11,899,400
1869.....	4,047	1,998,644	5,787,218	13,755,547	19,386	13,774,933
1870.....	4,082	2,135,993	5,995,121	15,305,040	158,888	15,463,928
1871.....	4,335	2,362,621	6,664,629	17,303,815	166,456	17,470,271
1872.....	4,607	2,745,245	7,699,916	19,559,804	301,070	19,860,874

Every year shows an increase in the number and amount of deposits; and on the 31st day of December, 1872, the total balances applicable to the payment of depositors amounted to the sum of £19,860,874. The postmaster-general states, in his last annual report, that the cost of each deposit or withdrawal, including postage, is now about sixpence instead of about one shilling in the old savings banks. No greater triumph was ever achieved in post-office management, with the single exception of that of Sir Rowland Hill, in effecting penny postage.

Post-office savings banks encountered at every step the most implacable opposition, and were established only after a prolonged struggle. The same arguments were brought to bear against them that have been used against the adoption of a like system here. It was urged that they would be destructive of the old savings banks; that the post-office would never be able to perform the additional important duties imposed upon it; that the Government was undertaking a great risk; and that the scheme was centralizing in its tendency. They were opposed by Lord Colchester, an ex-postmaster-general, and by Lord Monteagle, of Brandon, once chancellor of the exchequer. A practical trial of twelve years has conclusively established the fallacy of all the arguments adduced against this beneficent measure.

The same system, somewhat simplified, has been put into operation in the British Australian colonies, in Queensland, and in Canada, with like unvarying success. Mr. J. C. Stewart, superintendent of the post-office savings banks of Canada, writes, under date of October 25, 1873:

"Post-office savings banks work smoothly with us. We commenced five and a half years ago very much in the dark, and we have had to work out the system to a great extent unaided; but we learned to think out and reason out a system with which we are now well satisfied. There is nothing which prevents our extending it to every money-order office, save want of office accommodation at the head office."

Reason and philanthropy being thus sustained by the prolonged experience of so many people speaking the English language, how can the success of similar institutions in the United States be longer doubtful? I believe that the financial perils through which we are now passing could have been mainly averted if these institutions had been open to receive deposits. The people of this country earn more and deposit more than those of any other. The State of New York alone exhibits an aggregate of savings-bank deposits equal to those of the whole United Kingdom of Great Britain and Ireland; and it is not extravagant to say that if the spirit of the universal frugality could be encouraged by an assurance of good faith and absolute security, the savings of the American people would soon grow into such gigantic proportions that the voluntary loans of a single generation would exceed the whole of the national debt.

I am clear in the conviction that the establishment of postal savings depositories will be found an eminently wise and practical measure; and, in the hope of contributing something to that end, I will submit at an early day a form of bill embodying the necessary legislation.

HON. HORACE MAYNARD—1880.

POSTAL SAVINGS.

One of my predecessors some years since recommended the incorporation into the department of a system of postal savings. The subject has from time to time occupied the attention of Congress. For several years the system has been in operation in the United Kingdom of Great Britain and Ireland, and in Canada. When in London recently, Her Majesty's postmaster-general kindly gave me facilities for observing the management of his department. I learned that the postal savings system had been remarkably successful, and had constantly grown in popular favor. As managed in that country, it is a source of some profit to the Government.

In this country I incline to the belief that the system would have advantages even greater than in a compact population like that of Great Britain. The subject will be found intelligently discussed by a gentleman connected with the money-order office upon page 379, of the appendix.

Wealth, public and private, consists largely of the savings of production over consumption, small in detail, but enormous in the aggregate. In by far the larger portion of the United States there are no savings depositories, and are not likely to be. To the people of these parts the use of the post-office for this purpose would be a real boon. It would be an additional advantage that deposits would be available at any depository office in the United States, an important consideration with a people so migratory as ours. It is believed the system would interfere little with the business of the savings banks, but would absorb funds not now deposited in them. Nor would the patronage of the Government be sensibly increased, since the system would be operated by persons already in the public service, with no considerable addition to the number. Your attention and the attention of Congress is respectfully invited to it.

HON. T. L. JAMES—1881.

POSTAL SAVINGS DEPOSITORIES.

As early as 1871 a recommendation was made by one of my predecessors for the establishment of a system of savings depositories in connection with this Department, and in several subsequent annual reports this recommendation has been renewed.

December 18, 1873, "A bill to establish and maintain a national savings depository as a branch of the Post-Office Department" was introduced in the House of Representatives by Hon. Horace Maynard, of Tennessee. From time to time since that date the measure has occupied the attention of Congress, and many bills have been introduced, but without securing definite action.

A system of post-office savings banks went into operation in Great Britain September 16, 1861. At the close of its first complete year, the number of open accounts was 178,495, and the amount standing to the credit of depositors was £1,698,221, being an average of £9 10s. 3d. to each account. Since that time the institution has grown rapidly in popular favor, and on the 31st of December, 1879, the number of outstanding accounts had risen to 1,988,477, and the amount of the credit of depositors to £32,012,134, an average of £16 1s. 11¼d. to each. The interest paid to depositors is only 2½ per centum, a rate so low as practically to exclude the post-office savings banks from competition with other banking institutions, as the history of the rise and progress of savings institutions in Great Britain has demonstrated, the object of the government being to offer to the depositor security rather than profitable investment for his earnings, and to promote frugality, steady habits, and consequent thrift among the laboring classes.

My predecessor, in his last annual report, said that if the larger portion of the United States there are no savings depositories, and are not likely to be; and he expressed the opinion that, to the people of these parts, the use of the post-office for this purpose would be a real boon. That it would be an advantage to the patrons of the institution, that deposits would be available at any depository post-office in the country, "an important consideration with a people so migratory as ours." He further expressed the belief that the system would interfere little with the business of the savings banks, but would rather absorb funds not now deposited in them. He thought that the patronage of the Government would not be sensibly increased, since the system would be conducted by persons already in the public service, with no considerable addition to their number.

In these views I concur. It is my earnest conviction that a system of this description, if adopted, would inure more than almost any other measure of public importance to the benefit of the working people of the United States, and I commend it to the favorable consideration of Congress.

HON. T. O. HOWE—1882.

POSTAL SAVINGS BANKS.

I follow in the steps of many of my predecessors in this office when I invoke Congress to make one more effort to ingraft upon the postal service a system of deposits for small sums. The great lesson our people need to learn is that of economy. The American people are apt to earn but are not wise to save.

The easy introduction to the art of saving is to provide a convenient and safe means of saving. A lucrative means is less essential. A place near at hand where a dollar may be deposited and may be secure against the temptations of the burglar, the thief, and the saloon keeper, even if it accumulates but very little, has everywhere proved a strong inducement to saving. The post-office is near to every citizen; the savings bank must always be remote from the most. The post-office need not be a substitute for the savings bank, nor its rival, but its feeder; a place where small deposits with slow accretions may securely grow into large ones, then to be transferred to savings banks on longer terms and with larger earnings.

FROM THE REPORT OF THE POSTMASTER-GENERAL—1889.

POSTAL SAVINGS BANKS.

If the letters and arguments presented at the Department and articles in the newspapers are an evidence of interest in this subject there is a steadily growing sentiment in favor of the Government offering through the post-offices a depository for savings. Foreign countries have for many years past extended these conveniences for the people and good results are reported without exception.

The report of the Postmaster-General of Great Britain for 1889 says:

The growth of business in the savings bank has been exceptionally rapid during the year 1888. * * * The deposits in the year numbered 7,540,625, amounting to $95,261,130, as against 6,916,327 and $82,679,660, the number and amount for the year 1887. The withdrawals were 2,633,808 in number, amounting in all to $79,013,675, showing an increase of 137,514 in number and of $5,612,280 in amount over the number and amount for 1887. As a net result of these transactions, a total sum of $292,781,970, including interest, remained to the credit of depositors on the 31st December, 1888, being an increase of $22,911,645 for the year as compared with an increase of $15,498,635 in 1887. The amount of interest credited to depositors was $6,664,190 or $443,820 more than in 1887.

The greatest number of deposits on one day was 60,936, amounting to $907,445, and made on the 31st December. The greatest number of withdrawals on one day was 20,348, amounting to $446,985, made on the 18th December. The average amount of each deposit was £2 10s. 6d., as compared with £2 7s. 10d. in 1887. * * * The average amount of each withdrawal was £6, as compared with £5 17s. 7d. in 1887.

The number of accounts opened in 1888 was 887,460 and 618,294 were closed. The corresponding numbers for 1887 were, respectively, 794,592 and 574,252. The total number of accounts open at the end of the year was 4,220,927, distributed as follows:

	Number.	Proportion to population.	Average balance due to each depositor.
			£ s. d.
England and Wales	3,900,334	1 to 7	13 17 3
Scotland	148,288	1 to 27	8 8 11
Ireland	172,305	1 to 28	18 15 4

"The total number of post-offices open for the transaction of savings-bank business on the 31st December, 1888, was 9,022, or 302 more than in 1887, of which 254 were opened in England and Wales, 28 in Scotland, and 20 in Ireland."

The fact that over four millions of persons (4,220,927) in the kingdom of Great Britain alone take advantage of this means of security and saving is certainly significant. Not less so is the sum of nearly three hundred million of dollars ($292,781,070) to the credit of the depositors on January 1, 1889. But the amount of self-reliance, thrift, and good citizenship encouraged by this feature of the Government is beyond any calculation.

To connect more intimately countless numbers of citizens with this country is a patriotic service. It would tend to weaken incipient disturbances; it would aid in breaking down sectional feelings. The State and private savings banks in many of the States where small deposits can be made are comparatively few in number. In some parts of the country there are no such opportunities offered. The chimney corner, the trunk, the closet, and the old stocking hide another surplus, not unlike that heaped up in the Treasury; and practically it is as much withdrawn from circulation. To offer needed security to these millions striving to be provident, to encourage other m illions now thoughtlessly improvident, and bind closer to the nation all those who are benefited—men, women, and children alike—is worthy of the loftiest statesmanship.

The grave question at the threshold is what to do with the money deposited; how to put it into circulation and make it earn an interest. The claim sometimes made that for the Government to take up this business would be an interference with the banks and savings funds will not hold good. I maintain that the habits of saving engendered would be widely felt and increase the savings of all who are already depositors. Besides, but few of the existing institutions can afford to bestow their labor on receiving sums as small as those which the postal savings bank would invite. Fixing a limit to the amount of deposits at $150 from any one person in one year would tend to turn away from the post-office banks to other banks and savings funds the aggregated deposits as soon as sufficiently large to be desirable to financial institutions.

I suggest early consideration of the question of establishing postal savings banks at 10,000 of the fourth-class offices in towns where such facilities are most needed, leaving the extension of this privilege to be determined after a trial of 2 years. There are three plans: First, to accept limited deposits, upon which interest at the rate of not more than 2 per cent. be paid; second, if objection be made to the Government obligating itself to pay interest, accept deposits with an agreement to invest and distribute their earnings less one-eighth of 1 per cent. for the cost of the service; third, if it is deemed inadvisable to undertake any such obligation, offer the post-offices as depositaries without interest, affording the people the convenience and safety. In each case the Secretary of the Treasury would loan the money, equitably distributing it to the banks in the States where the deposits originated to keep it in circulation, requiring United States bonds as security, and interest, if the Government pays interest, but not otherwise.

The suggestion of a modified plan for small savings is made in case the other plans are disapproved; that authority be given to the Department to redeem for cash, under regulations prescribed by the Postmaster-General, all undefaced postage stamps or postal cards when presented at any post-office on savings cards in multiples of $1. While this would be the least important of the four schemes, I believe it would find a hearty response among the toiling people, especially the younger and smaller wage-earners.

FROM THE REPORT OF THE POSTMASTER-GENERAL, 1890.

SAVINGS BANKS AT POST-OFFICES.

The Post-Office Department is continually urged to act as the guardian of moneys for people resident in parts of the country where savings banks do not exist. It is not the large cities that feel this need, though even at the populous centers banking institutions generally do not offer convenient hours for working people and do not care to deal with small sums. It is the large mass of wage-earners outside of large cities that clamor for help to keep hard-earned gains. In some of the States no laws exist to give State protection to savings deposited with private capitalists.' It is stated on reputable authority that in one portion of the country containing twelve millions of population there are not as many places of deposit for the saving of small sums as exist in a single city of 80,000 people in a New England State.

To teach economy and thrift as leading up to better citizenship falls short if there is no adequate provision for the safe-keeping of savings. Such places ought to be within an hour's walk of the home of every workingman. They can not be left to private capitalists to provide, because it would not pay them to deal in small sums or perform the necessary labor. The post-offices and the postmasters are in every respect rightly situated to do this work. It would be a great comfort to the people to have these banks that could not be affected in times of financial panic.

Of all the great powers in the world the United States and Germany alone are without postal savings systems. The last report of the British authorities shows that on the average 1 person out of every 8 in the United Kindom is a depositor in the postal savings, and while in England and Wales the average balance to each depositor is almost $70, in Ireland, where the conditions are harder, the average balance to each depositor is close to $94, owing doubtless to fewer opportunities to invest or deposit money for safe-keeping.

In Mr. Lacey's report to the Forty-seventh Congress, urging the establishment of postal savings banks, he quotes as follows from the twenty-sixth report of the postmaster-general of the United Kingdom:

"Notwithstanding the dullness of trade and the deficiency of the harvest that characterized the year 1879, it is satisfactory to report a continued excess of deposits over withdrawals and an increase in the balance due to depositors of upwards of a million and a half sterling. Most remarkable, perhaps, is the progress shown in Ireland, considering the severe distress to which many parts of that country have been subject. For the whole of Ireland there was, including interest, an increase in the balance due to depositors of $457,915, and of this amount the eight counties chiefly affected by the distress contributed no less than $127,090."

The Postmaster-General of Great Britain states in his last report that the number of savings bank depositors last year was 8,101,120, an increase of 560,495 persons, and that the total amount of deposits for the year was a fraction under $100,000,000, nearly $4,000,000 more than the previous year. In one day over 55,000 persons made deposits amounting to over $685,000. There were 924,010 new accounts opened in 1889 and 637,128 closed. The total number of open active accounts at the end of the year was 4,507,809, or nearly 300,000 more than the previous year. The report gives interesting data of the growth of the savings system in the British provinces. In Ceylon the system was established in 1885, and "proved a boon to the poorer population."

An interesting statement in the Bankers' Monthly for October says:

"But the greatest extension of savings banks has been brought about by the introduction of the system of post-office banks. In India, as in England, the use of the already existing machinery of the post-office has not only proved of the greatest advantage in point of economy of administration, but has been of the utmost service in extending the opportunity of profitably exercising thrift into many parts of the country where otherwise it would be impossible to afford such accommodations without incurring a cost too great to be borne by the business of the district. * * * In March, 1888, the totals of accounts and balances in the various savings banks were as follows:

	Accounts.	Balances.
		Rupees,
3 presidency banks..	39,403	11,518,734
12 railway banks..	12,848	2,295,501
170 military banks	18,303	1,473,783
5,966 post-office banks..	261,157	50,488,357
Total...	331,711	65,777,375

The last French report at hand is that of 1885, which shows the amount of deposits to be over $53,000,000. In Belgium the depositors at the close of 1888 had $50,000,000 to their credit. In the Netherlands the deposits were upwards of $5,800,000. In Sweden at the close of 1887, the depositors, 59 per cent. of whom were minors, had $766,430 to their credit. Comparison of the deposits in 1887 with those of 1884 shows an increase of over 100 per cent. A report of the postmaster-general of the Hawaiian Kingdom dated February 11, 1890, shows that that country first had postal savings in 1886, and has now 2,641 depositors with $909,613 on deposit, against $477,475 one year before. It would seem as though the United States should not be the last country to offer assistance to the masses of her people struggling to rise by thrift and economy.

I recommend that the Post-Office Department be authorized to establish postal savings banks under regulations formulated by the Postmaster-General; that the said banks be located as follows: (1) In States having no laws regulating savings banks; (2) in any other States upon petition of a considerable number of residents of any one locality; and (3) not more numerously than one post-office for every 10 miles of area; that the interest to be paid depositors shall be fixed by the Secretary of the Treasury at the beginning of each year, and be one-half of 1 per cent. less than the average rate paid to depositors by private bankers; that all postal savings received within a State shall be placed on deposit with the national banks of that State, on application, in such amounts and at such interest as the Secretary of the Treasury shall prescribe, and that all such deposits be declared by special enactment preferred claims against the banks holding them.

Exhibit 4.

SUMMARY OF THE EFFORTS TO PROVIDE LEGISLATION ON THE SUBJECT OF POSTAL SAVINGS BANKS.

IN THE HOUSE OF REPRESENTATIVES.

Date.	No. of bill.	Title of bill.	Introduced or reported by—
Dec. 18, 1873	797	To establish and maintain a national savings depository as a branch of the Post-Office Department.	Mr. Maynard.
Oct. 29, 1877	548	....do	Mr. Tipton.
Mar. 15, 1878	3848	To promote the refunding of the national debt and the loan of the savings to the United States for that purpose.	Mr. Robbins.
Mar. 21, 1878	3989	To establish a postal savings depository as a branch of the Post-Office Department and to aid in refunding the interest-bearing indebtedness of the United States.	Mr. Waddell.
Apr. 17, 1879	4395	To provide for the deposit of savings in a popular loan and to provide for funding the national debt in home bonds convertible into currency.	Mr. Phillips.
Dec. 16, 1881	850	To establish and maintain a postal savings depository as a branch of the Post-Office Department.	Mr. Money.
Feb. 8, 1882	4198	To establish a postal savings depository as a branch of the Post-Office Department.	Mr. Lacey.
Dec. 11, 1883	812	....do...	Do.
Do.......	897	....do...	Mr. O'Neill.
Mar. 16, 1886	6746	To establish post-office savings banks as a branch of the Post-Office Department.	Mr. McComas.

IN THE SENATE.

Date.	No. of bill.	Title of bill.	Introduced or reported by—
Mar. 13, 1878	917	To promote the deposit of savings and the refunding of the national debt.	Mr. Gordon.
Feb. 24, 1886	1622	To establish a postal savings depository as a branch of the Post-Office Department.	Mr. Miller.

EXTRACTS FROM A REPORT SUBMITTED FEBRUARY 21, 1882, BY MR. LACEY, FROM THE COMMITTEE ON THE POST-OFFICE AND POST-ROADS OF THE HOUSE OF REPRESENTATIVES.

POSTAL SAVINGS DEPOSITORIES.

FEBRUARY 21, 1882.—Referred to the House Calendar and ordered to be printed.

Mr. LACEY, from the Committee on the Post-Office and Post-Roads, submitted the following report (to accompany bill H. R. 4198).

The Committee on the Post-Office and Post-Roads, to whom was referred the bill (H. R. 4198) relating to the establishment of a postal savings depository as a branch of the Post-Office Department, submit the same with amendments, and make the following report:

Since the beginning of the present century the philanthropists of all nations have been earnestly endeavoring to promote the establishment of institutions for savings, and the great and beneficial influence exerted upon the laboring classes for their elevation and improvement, by these agencies, is sufficient proof that their efforts have been wisely directed. To provide safe and convenient institutions for this purpose should be the aim of every wise legislator. Whatever can be as well done by

43

private enterprise as by the Government should never be entered upon by the latter, and it is far from the purpose of your committee to supersede or interfere with sound banks now or hereafter organized by private enterprise under State authority; but we are of the opinion that private enterprise alone does not, and can not, in this respect, meet the necessities of the industrious poor in any country, and least of all in the United States.

The New England States, having a dense population conveniently clustered about mills and factories, is, in a greater degree than other parts of the Union, supplied with these institutions, averaging 1 to every 9,436 inhabitants, and so long as these banks are well and successfully managed the proposed system will in no degree interfere with their business.

But the remaining thirty-two States have but one savings bank to every 225,000 people. To supply these 46,000,000 people as well as are now those of New England we should need 5,000 savings banks instead of 236, which is the present number.

On the 30th of June, 1881, there were 5,499 money-order post-offices in the United States, and if the Postmaster-General were to designate all of these as subdepositories under this act, the people of the whole country would be no better accommodated in point of numbers than is now the population of New England. It is impossible for private enterprise to supply this want. It is possible for the Government. Its offices are already open at the exact places where this business can be most conveniently transacted; it has in each of these offices a corps of officers especially adapted to the purpose; it has excellent facilities for transporting the deposits to a common center for investment, and is itself a borrower at a higher rate of interest than is to be paid the depositor under this act.

All power under our form of government comes from the people—an aggregation of individual voters. If these are vicious and unthrifty, bad government and finally utter failure must follow. Idleness results in poverty and vice. Industry is promoted by increasing the facility and certainty with which its fruits may be preserved and enjoyed. An industrious, frugal, thrifty man is rarely a bad citizen, and good citizenship insures a wise and stable government.

In the light of these facts, and the great success which has attended the establishment of the postal savings system in other countries, your committee cannot give much weight to objections based upon mere theories—objections which have been repeatedly met and overcome abroad by the stern logic of actual experience.

*   *   *   *   *

The bill under consideration provides in substance that none but money-order post-offices can be authorized to receive deposits.

No single deposit can be less than ten cents nor more than one hundred dollars.

No more than one hundred dollars can be deposited by one person within any period of thirty days.

The amount due a depositor is limited to five hundred dollars.

Money deposited is to be immediately forwarded to some Government depository by the postmaster who receives it, and invested by the Secretary of the Treasury in interest-bearing securities issued or guarantied by the United States, and if these can not be purchased without loss to the depository then in approved State securities.

The account of each depositor is to be kept at the central depository in Washington, where interest at the rate of two per cent. per annum is computed and credited.

All withdrawals are by checks issued under the authority of the Postmaster-General.

The expenses of the system are to be paid from the profits of the business.

Your committee believe the provisions of this bill to be wise, and that by its operations both the depositor and the Government would be mutually benefited. We also believe that this business can properly be conducted by the Post-Office Department. The latter is now engaged in carrying merchandise and selling exchange for the sole purpose of adding to the commercial facilities of the people, while the system hereby proposed will not alone prove a great convenience, but will elevate the standard of citizenship and largely promote the prosperity and happiness of all.

Recognizing the obligations which we as legislators owe to that numerous class upon whose industry, frugality, and resulting virtues the prosperity of our country and the permanence of its institutions must at all times rest, we believe all technical objections which stand in the way of their best interests should be swept aside, and that the welfare of these, the industrious poor, the producing millions of our land, should be given paramount consideration.

We therefore recommend the passage of the bill as amended.

Exhibit 5.

In the Senate of the United States,
December 11, 1890.
 Resolved, That the Committee on Post Offices and Post-Roads be, and it is hereby, instructed to inquire into the feasibility and advisability of the enactment of a law creating postal savings banks in connection with all or certain classes of post-offices throughout the country, and to report by bill or otherwise at the present session.
 Attest: ANSON G. McCOOK,
                   Secretary

45

Exhibit 6.

PRESS COMMENTS CONCERNING POSTAL SAVINGS BANKS.

1. Favorable to their establishment.
2. Against their establishment.

FAVORABLE TO POSTAL SAVINGS BANKS.

[American Banker, New York, September 6, 1890.]

A FEW WORDS ABOUT POST-OFFICE SAVINGS BANKS.

[Read before the American Social Science Association, by J. H. Thiry, of Long Island City, N. Y.]

The European system of post-office savings banks has recently occupied the attention of the press, reformers, scientists, economists, philanthropists, and even a large number of educators of our country. In 1882 a bill was presented in the legislature favoring their introduction, but for some reason or other it was not approved. "Other time other customs." Eight years or more of experience has probably changed the attitude of the legislature. To-day *ignorance, intemperance,* and *improvidence,* according to popular declaration, are the three worst foes to American social progress. Our public schools can cure *ignorance,* a proper education will lessen the follies of *intemperance,* and the habits of thrift and economy, properly taught to our children, will reduce considerably the number of *improvidents.*

Compulsory education will reduce ignorance, as Shakespeare says: "Ignorance is the curse of God; knowledge the wing wherewith we fly to heaven."

Manual training and the lessons of thrift and economy taught to our children will prove a means of reducing intemperance, for "A drunkard's purse is a bottle," and, to quote Bacon: "All the crimes on earth do not destroy so many of the human race nor alienate so much property as drunkenness." The habit of saving inculcated in the scholars according to the system which has been on trial during the last 5 years in the 112 schools of our country, will serve as an incentive to temperance and as a preventive to improvidence. "One hand washes the other, and both the face."

Can the European system of post-office savings banks, with its complicated machinery, its heavy expenses, help us? I do not see it. A close survey of our customs, our form of government, the topography of all the regions of the domain of Uncle Sam, compared with that of the European nations, force the conclusion that on account of the large amount of labor, expense, and inconvenience, its introduction would not warrant an adequate return. However, from a careful examination of all the plans suggested thus far, only two appear to meet the wants of our time and country, and they have been proposed by Hon. Horace J. Smith, of Philadelphia, one of the most earnest and best-informed advocates of the post-office savings-bank system in America. In a contribution to the Statesman of Chicago, Ill., Mr. Smith's outline of the plans runs as follows:

First plan.—"That the savings of the people, deposited at the post-offices, instead of being centralized in the Treasury in Washington, should remain in the State in which they originate." * * *

Second plan.—"That the savings of the people, deposited at the post-offices, should be transmitted to the nearest national or savings bank, under the particular scrutiny of the Government to preclude almost any possibility of loss." * * *

According to my view the second plan is the one that will be found the most satisfactory, without entailing great labors, inconvenience, and expense, and the one which, above all, would most readily meet with popular acceptance. In the localities where savings banks could not possibly be established the post-offices would become an agent for the receipt and transmission of the savings of the people and be the intermediary agent between the teachers and the regular banking institution which would accept the totals.

46

In case such a plan should receive the approbation of all concerned, the next thing needed is a reduction of the usual rates for transportation of the funds (deposits and withdrawals) from one place to another. From the writer's experience and that of many of those with whom he has been in correspondence during the last four years, the practical working of the plan, under a wise code of legislation, would prove a great boon for those dwelling in sections where the art of saving is unknown. Those of us who have seen this system in operation and studied its results trust sincerely that our legislators will soon recognize the wisdom of sanctioning its adoption in our own country.

The rules and regulations of the school savings-bank system will be published in full in a future issue of The American Banker. Parties interested and desiring copies of same are requested to send in applications to this office at an early date.

[Indianapolis News, Sept. 30.]

Penny-savings institutions are to be established in Boston on a plan essentially the same as the British Postal Savings Bank. The purpose is to afford the poor a convenient means of saving small sums. No interest will be paid, as the income from such investments as can be made will not be larger than the expense of handling the funds. The benefits to be derived from the system are largely more than the money that can be saved. That is not likely, in any case, to grow into a sum sufficient to more than tide the depositor over some short period of misfortune. The inculcation of the habit of saving is the important thing. It develops thrift and is the surest way of checking pauperism. The person who learns to save has learned the first lesson of success. All the knowledge that can be gained from schools and colleges is not, to the person who must be self-dependent worth as much as knowledge of how to save and the habit of doing it. It is the foundation of all fortunes. It is the best safeguard against intemperance and immorality. The savings institutions, among which we count in Indianapolis the building and loan associations, have done as much, if not more, to check the drinking habit than the temperance movements. Throughout the world it will be found that, in those countries where there is frugality, there is also the highest average of morality.

[Defiance (Ohio) Crescent, October 1, 1890.]

The question of post-office savings banks is an interesting one, and the plan is destined, no doubt, to be adopted in this country. Japan will teach us something when we begin, for, according to an article in a native journal, they were established by the Government in 1875, with the object of encouraging thrift and to collect the small sums scattered about in private keeping. At first they attracted so little attention that at the end of 1875 there were only 2,000 depositors, with $15,320 lodged. Henceforth, however, the figures increased at a remarkable rate. In 1876 the deposits amounted to $41,845, in 1882 to $1,058,000, in 1882 to $9,050,000, and in 1889 to $20,451,000. In Tokio the number of depositors is 356,000, and the amount of their deposits is $10,400,000. It is believed that the poorest people are not depositors, inasmuch as during the recent distress, due to comparative failure of the rice corn, the bulk of the deposits has undergone no diminution.

[Camden (N. J.) Gazette, October 4, 1890.]

Postal-savings banks are a means by which the Government offers through the post-office a depository for savings. To every citizen of the country, no matter where he may reside, provided he is within reach of some post-office which is a depository, the Government extends the opportunity to lay by his savings in small sums, allows interest thereon, and pledges its credit as security for their repayment on demand of the depositor or his representative.

They are not intended to interfere with or be a substitute for existing savings institutions, which for the most part deal with much larger sums and are found only in the larger centers of population, and chiefly in New England and the Middle Atlantic States, but to extend a privilege similar to that which private institutions afford to the very large class of small wage earners, many of whom live entirely out of reach of such institutions—on the principle that if saving and a place where what is saved can be kept in safety are good for some people they are good for all, and that the Government, being security, if anything in the country can be, and having already its "posts" established all over the land, should be the agent to furnish such facilities to its people.—Youth's Companion.

[Lowell (Mass.) News, October 6, 1890.]

PENNY SAVINGS.

Penny savings institutions are to be established in Boston on a plan essentially the same as the British postal savings bank. The plan is an admirable one. The purpose is to afford the poor a convenient means of saving small sums. No interest will be paid, as the income from such investments as can be made will not be larger than the expense of handling the funds. The benefits to be derived from the system are largely more than the money that can be saved. This is not likely in any case to grow into a sum sufficient to more than tide the depositor over some short period of misfortune. The inculcation of the habit of saving is the important thing. It develops thrift, and is the surest way of checking pauperism. The person who learns to save has learned the first lesson of success. All the knowledge that can be gained from schools and colleges is not, to the person who must be self-dependent, worth as much as knowledge of how to save and the habit of doing it. It is the foundation of all fortunes. It is the best safeguard against intemperance and immorality. The savings institutions, among which we count in Lowell, the building and loan association, has done as much, if not more, to check the drinking habit than the temperance movements. Throughout the world it will be found that in those countries where there is frugality, there is also the highest average of morality.

[Philadelphia Press, October 10, 1890.]

THRIFT WITH THE PENNIES.

[From the Boston Herald.]

The system of penny savings banks in schools is especially popular in Pennsylvania, where it includes the schools of Pottstown, Norristown, Chester, and Wilkes Barre. It has even spread to McCook, Lincoln, and Juniata, in the far-off Nebraska, Orangeburgh in South Carolina, and Harrisonburgh in Virginia. Capt. R. H. Pratt has incorporated it into his training school for Indians at Carlisle, Pa.

To sum up the development of this idea, in May, 1890, there were in the United States 114 schools which have adopted the system, working with 770 school savings banks. From a register of 38,527 pupils in the 114 schools, of 31 cities, 18,101 are depositors of the sum of $93,676.15, of which $30,221.61 has been withdrawn, leaving a balance of $63,454.54 due depositors.

THE PLAN PURSUED.

These schools pursue practically the same plan. The children bring their money every Monday morning; the teacher receives it, credits the amount on the child's card, which is about 6 by 4 inches, folded once. The teachers deliver the money received to the principal, who deposits it in the savings bank the same day. When a child has a deposit of 50 cents or more he gets a bank book, and when his deposits reach $3 and over, he gets interest quarterly. The principal keeps the bank books, and surrenders them to the children only in the presence of one parent. During the summer vacation the cashier of the bank conducts the business for the teachers.

According to the report for 1887 of the Bureau of Education at Washington, there are in the States and Territories 12,000,000 of school children. Taking the amounts already deposited as a basis, if penny banks had been organized in all the schools the children would have saved $25,250,000. Where has this large sum gone ?

One benefit resulting from the school savings of the child is the sympathetic influence of juvenile thrift on parental recklessness. Many a father is shamed into saving by the enthusiasm of his little boy. It is asserted that the banks would not handle the school money alone, but they find that a large number of parents go to the banks where the children's money is and open accounts of their own. This induces the banks to supply cards and receive the school deposits.

POSTAL-STAMP SAVINGS.

A national system of postal-stamp savings, or the universal adoption of school savings, would obviate further effort. In lieu of this, and to meet an urgent necessity, private helpfulness has established expedients to entice the poor to save very small sums.

Baltimore led the way by an adaptation of the British postal-stamp savings system, giving each depositor a bright-colored stamp as receipt. These are pasted on a pink card, where squares are marked out for 36 stamps. None of the savings banks were willing to coöperate efficiently, so the enterprising committee in charge established a savings bank under their own supervision.

Encouraged by the success in Baltimore, a penny provident fund was established in New York City by the Charity Organization Society. After having been in operation about a year, it was found, on November 1, 1889, that there was 8,846 depositors, aggregating $3,600.38. Slowly gaining the confidence of the community, the fund had, July 1, 1890, the sum of $7,014.77 remaining on deposit, and over 15,000 persons had availed themselves of the privilege in sums varying from 1 cent upward.

As was expected, the system is popular among the children. The different denominations of stamps bear different colors—1 cent, yellow; 3 cents, blue; 5 cents, green; 10 cents, brown; 25 cents, red; 50 cents, purple, and the young people seem to find the gay colors quite fascinating.

The business of this penny provident fund now includes over 75 branch stations in New York City. Besides the 10 district offices of the Charity Organization Society, stations are established at church missions, guilds, and Sunday schools, working girls' clubs, boys' industrial schools, and other places, gathering many earners of small wages. The United States Savings Bank on East Fifty-ninth street has also become a branch station, and in a short time numbered over 2,000 penny depositors.

The stability of this fund is assured by the high character of the society which established it, and the immediate supervision is conducted by a committee of gentlemen prominent in philanthropy and banking, and the treasurer gives a bond of $10,000 for the faithful discharge of his duty.

PENNY ECONOMIES.

On June of this year Detroit, Mich., began the system of penny savings, in what seems to be the wisest and most suitable way. The savings banks are very slow to adopt the stamp system as part of their business. In many cities banks have been urged to make it supplementary, but almost uniformly they give the project a cold shoulder. It is worth noting, however, that an enterprising bank in Lynn is considering the matter favorably.

Detroit is the first city to have a stamp savings attachment to a corporate bank. This bank was established in 1840, and has grown with the city. The cards, supplied by the banks, free of charge, are folded twice and put into an envelope 5 by 3 inches. Cards for the reception of 5-cent tokens are printed in red ink to correspond with the color of tokens themselves, the 10-cent tokens in green, the 25-cent in blue, and the 50-cent in black. Only those of one denomination are allowed on the same card. Each card has spaces marked off for twenty stamps, and when filled, the color at once indicates its value—the red $1; the green, $2; the blue, $5, and the black, $10. By this method the depositor chooses one of the six amounts represented by the token, and deposits it each time.

When a card is full, even the one whose face value is a dollar, it is put in the bank to draw interest, and the depositor receives a regular bank book, but he is at liberty to go on filling cards. The system now numbers about twenty-five agencies, established at drug stores and other responsible places, in various sections of the city. Although it has been in operation only three months, the results have fully equaled the expectations.

Boston is on the eve of an experiment to encourage small savings. The preliminary steps were taken in June, and an organization formed, called the stamp-saving society. One of the main objects of the promoters is to educate small wage-earners to place their small savings in a reliable bank. The society intends to serve as the channel through which these savings may be conveyed to the corporate banks, and in its main features follows the New York system. The central station will be opened for business October 15, at 36 Bromfield street. This is the headquarters for supplies and information, and the cashier will be in attendance from 2 to 4 o'clock every week day afternoon, excepting Saturday. This central station supplies branch stations with cards, and sells the necessary stamps, but does not sell to individual depositors. This is done only at the branch stations.

BOSTON'S SYSTEM.

Suppose a child wants to begin saving with 5 cents. He goes to the nearest branch office and receives a card numbered, dated, and marked with the name of the station issuing it. He signs his name for purposes of identification. He is given a 5-cent stamp as receipt for his money, and he affixes it to the first square of his card. Whenever he can save a few cents he takes his card to the station and gets another stamp on it. When the card is full he goes to the station where he received it and gets the face value, signing the card, which is retained at the station as voucher that he has received the money. This he can deposit in a savings bank, or the central office will supply him with a pass book. Minor changes may possibly be made before the society begins its business, but the depositor's card will bear substantially the following rules :

(1) Deposits are made only by attaching our stamps to this card. When one card is filled, ask for another. When a card is filled, or the sum of all the stamps attached amounts to $3 or more, the amount may be transferred to a pass book on delivery of the stamp card at the central office.

(2) Money can be withdrawn only upon presentation and surrender of this card at the stamp station, where the deposits are made, and one week's notice of intention to withdraw money may be required. No sum can be withdrawn less than the amount represented by all stamps attached. Stamps will be redeemed only when attached to a stamp card.

(3) If this card is lost or destroyed no payment will be made thereon.

(4) The fund is not a savings bank, but only an agency for the deposit of small savings. It is only responsible for the deposits of all moneys received by it in some trust company, savings banks, or other institution duly authorized by law to receive trust funds ; it is not responsible for any default of such depository.

(5) Every deposit is made and accepted subject to the above rules and conditions.

Readers will be glad to know that a sum as small as $10 is sufficient to start a branch station. The bookkeeping is reduced to a minimum by means of the stamps. There is little chance for trickery, as a branch must always have the value of its purchase at the central station, either in stamps, canceled stamps on cards, or cash. All the money received at the central station will be placed in a trust company, subject to the treasurer's order. Depositors get no interest until their money reaches the savings banks—the goal of their efforts.

In many respects this is one of the most important steps ever taken in Boston for the benefit of the industrial classes. The poor, the children, have, close at hand, a new stimulus to save even the smallest sums, and thus lay the foundations of future prosperity.

[Newville (Pa.) Star and Enterprise, October 16, 1890.]

Postal savings banks are a means by which the Government offers through the post-office a depository for savings. To every citizen of the country, no matter where he may reside, provided he is within reach of some post-office which is a depository, the Government extends the opportunity to lay by his savings in small savings in small sums, allows interest thereon, and pledges its credit as security for the repayment on demand of the depositor or his representative.

They are not intended to interfere with or be a substitute for existing savings institutions, which for the most part deal with much larger sums and are found in the larger centers of population, and chiefly in the New England and Middle Atlantic States; but to extend a privilege similar to that which private institutions afford to the very large class of small wage-earners, many of whom live entirely out of reach of such institutions—on the principle that if saving and a place where what is saved can be kept in safety are good for some people they are good for all, and that the Government, being security, if anything in the country can be, and having already its "posts" established all over the land, should be the agent to furnish such facilities to its people.

[Portland (Me.) Express, November 25, 1890.]

It is announced that Postmaster-General Wanamaker, in his annual report, will outline a plan of postal savings banks in connection with the smaller post-offices of the country in places where these banks will not interfere with local savings institutions. Mr. Wanamaker expresses his belief, and certainly the success of a similar plan in England supports him, that such a plan would prove a great blessing to the poor and would teach them habits of saving which would not only benefit them, but benefit the country.

He does not believe that the Government will for several years make any reduction in the rate of postage on the ground that this important branch of the Government ought to be self-sustaining, while as a matter of fact, even with 2-cent postage, there is an annual deficit of about $6,000,000. It is a mistaken policy to limit the facilities of extending and improving the mail facilities of this country solely to make the Post-Office Department self-sustaining.

If this principle was carried out in all branches of the National Government the United States would cut a pitiable figure among the nations of the world. Cheaper postage is a necessity for the expansion of business communications, and the revenues would be largely increased by the adoption of penny postage.

[Philadelphia Bulletin, November 25.]

Mr. Wanamaker is still a firm believer in postal savings banks, and will advocate them in his forthcoming report. It seems, however, that he would use them as an adjunct to and not a rival of the savings banks of the cities, and would, therefore, establish them principally at county post-offices where there are no other depositaries of small sums. No doubt they would be highly useful there.

[Philadelphia North American, November 26.]

Why Congress should need so much urging to establish the postal savings-bank system in the United States is not quite clear. Mr. Wanamaker discusses the subject in his current report and earnestly recommends the system, but other post-office officials have done that before him, and their recommendations have been calmly ignored. Yet the arguments are really all on one side. There are any number of good reasons why we should have postal savings banks in this country, and there is no reason at all to the contrary. In Great Britain, where the postal-saving system has been in operation for many years, its success has been unqualified. It has been of incalculable benefit to the community as an agency for the promotion of thrift, and has proved in every way a public convenience of extraordinary value. Its advantages are that it is absolutely safe, that it encourages the man who can only save a very little to put that little away, and that it enables him to deposit or withdraw his money at any post-office in the United Kingdom where he may happen to be. These are three important points in favor of the system, which could as well be carried on in the United States as it is in Great Britain. It is strange that Congress should be so slow to recognize its merits.

[Troy Standard, November 26.]

The Postmaster-General's suggestions to Congress are evidently worthy of consideration. It is to be hoped that, taking a lesson from the late election the Fifty-first Congress, in its closing session, will inaugurate a popular policy. This offers the only prospect of making any immediate impression upon the people that will be favorable to the Republican party. The Democrats are soon to have their opportunity, and well will it be for their party if they display not that capacity for blundering which has been for years past the curse of their party. The Republicans are no better in principle, so far as their Congressional Representatives are concerned. Their subserviency to great railroad and telegraph monopolies more than anything else has tended to reduce them to the pitiable plight in which they now find themselves. The marvel of it all is that as a rule the professional politician on neither side sees this. He goes muttering and grumbling of free trade or protection to his post as if either the one or the other must constitute the sole popular interest in politics, and in short determine the rise and fall of parties. Perhaps the Farmers' Alliance members of Congress can teach him something under this head. Let them show the professional politician that any programme that will satisfy the people must be a broad one.

It is to the credit of the administrative officers of the Government that they have shown more discernment than the Congressmen. While Postmaster-General Wanamaker is repeating for the hundredth time, more or less, his postal-telegraph and postal-savings bank recommendations, Secretary Windom is equally solicitous in behalf of measures that would contribute to swell the volume and stability of the currency. This project of the Secretary, who is in line with his previous record in regard to this policy, coincides with the views of the farmers. Some of the latter have spoken more or less of the tariff, but it is apparent that their views under this head are not unanimous, while the currency question finds them practically a unit in opinion.

Just at this juncture, too, the Postmaster-General's views of the savings project would suit them nicely. Private banks, especially with people of no extensive financial experience, are with reason distrusted. A Government bank could never fail in a Republic to the extent of being beyond power to pay its depositors. This is but one of the arguments that may be adduced in favor of such an institution, but it is all-sufficient, albeit the incidental benefits of post-office banking would be many and widespread.

[Philadelphia Call, November 26.]

A great many things can be said in favor of a postal-savings bank system and nothing can be said against it. Postmaster-General Wanamaker's recommendation ought to be adopted by Congress.

[Philadelphia (Pa.) Journal, November 26.]

The Postmaster-General has matured his report of the Post-Office Department, a portion of which being of the most vital interest to the wage-earning class of the community. He has already championed the postal telegraph question, and his views thereon are fairly well known.

Post-office savings banks has occupied a large share of attention, and his report thereon, which will shortly be given to the country, will be found of the utmost importance. This subject has found great favor with Postmaster-General Wanamaker, and undoubtedly he has made the working of this important institution in England, which has proven a great success, a matter of deep study and close investigation. The establishing of the post-office savings banks will enable the humblest citizen to have a safe place of deposit for small amounts, and especially will the advantage be found in scattered and small outlying communities where no banks are to be found within a radius of several miles. It will be found an encourager of thrift and economy, and millions of dollars now needlessly wasted for the want of proper protection will thus be saved. It is well known that vast sums of money are now lying idle in cupboards, in old stockings, and other hiding places, but with the establishment of the post-office savings banks, these amounts may be added to the circulating medium of the country.

In England there are over 250 millions of dollars in the post-office savings banks to the credit of the working class, who deposit from a quarter upwards. These depositors can make any post-office in the United Kingdom their bank, where they can both deposit their money and withdraw it; so that if away from home and desire to put any money into safe custody all the depositor has to do is to go into the nearest post-office, or branch bank, deposit the money and present the passbook that the amount might be entered therein. The official stamp with date is placed against the amount, as also the initials of the clerk or postmaster. By return of post a letter is received from London by the depositor informing him that the amount has been placed to his credit. Should the depositor desire to withdraw an amount he or she can go into any post-office, put the amount required on a slip of paper with his or her signature, and by return of post an order is received by the office from which it is desired to receive it to pay the amount asked for. Interest at the rate of 2½ per cent. is given, and the passbooks are balanced half yearly.

Such a system in this country will be of incalculable value, and Postmaster-General Wanamaker will deserve the best thanks of the wage-earners especially for the great boon.

[Philadelphia Inquirer, November 26.]

There will be one advantage about Mr. Wanamaker's postal-savings banks, if established: They are not likely to be affected by financial panics.

[Shenandoah (Pa.) Herald, November 28.]

The Philadelphia North American can not understand why Congress should need so much urging to establish the postal-savings bank system in the United States is not quite clear. Mr. Wanamaker discusses the subject in his current report and earnestly recommends the system, but other post-office officials have done that before him, and their recommendations have been calmly ignored. Yet the arguments are really all on one side. There are any number of good reasons why we should have postal savings banks in this country, and there is no reason at all to the contrary. In Great Britain, where the postal savings system has been in operation for many years, its success has been unqualified. It has been of incalculable benefit to the community as an agency for the promotion of thrift, and has proved in every way a public convenience of extraordinary value. Its advantages are that it is absolutely safe, that it encourages the man who can only save a very little to put that little away, and that it enables him to deposit or withdraw his money at any post-office in the United Kingdom where he may happen to be. These are three important points in favor of the system, which could as well be carried on in the United States as it is in Great Britain. It is strange that Congress should be so slow to recognize its merits.

[Philipsburgh (Pa.) Journal, November 28, 1890.]

Such a system in this country will be of incalculable value, and Postmaster-General Wanamaker will deserve the best thanks of the wage-earners especially for the great boon,

[Omaha (Nebr.) Bee, November 29, 1890.]

POSTAL SAVINGS BANKS.

Postmaster-General Wanamaker appears to be sincerely ambitious to make his term in office memorable by giving the people new and permanent benefits. Among the various progressive reforms he has suggested perhaps none is more capable of doing great good than the establishment of postal savings banks.

Mr. Wanamaker's plan is to have savings banks instituted in connection with post-offices wherever they are called for by popular petitions. He states that he will take care not to bring them into competition with savings banks that already exist or with building loan associations. He believes a sum that would aggregate a vast total is secreted in all sorts of out-of-the-way places by a class of people who are afraid of banking institutions, and that his proposition would be the means of bringing it into circulation, with advantage to the business public.

The great benefit which may be expected from the successful establishment of postal-savings banks, however, will be its effects on the habits of the people. If these institutions can be made popular we shall see the beginning of a new era of thrift among the classes which stand most in need of it. When a savings bank can be found at every little post-office, people who have not formerly been in the habit of systematically accumulating money will begin to do so. There will be a revival of the good old-fashioned custom of saving instead of spending the surplus income, and the fact that the surplus is small will not deter people from laying it by where it will grow. It is the prevalence and popularity of savings banks which has made the wage-workers of New England the thriftiest class of working people in the world. It is the lack of such facilities, almost as much as the lack of proper teachings, which has led the people in other sections of the country away from habits of frugality and thrift. It is not necessary to enlarge on the inestimable advantage of general thrift among the people to demonstrate the great possibilities of good which may follow the establishment of postal-savings banks and the consequent revival of the soundest household maxims among the young men and women of the country.

If, in addition to the introduction of business methods in the service and the inauguration of a system of postal telegraphy, John Wanamaker gives the people popular savings banks, he will have done his part to make President Harrison's administration " great in the arduous greatness of things done."

[St. Louis Sayings, November 29.]

The necessity of postal-savings banks has long been recognized, and it will be in order for the Government to grant the boon in as simple and business-like a manner as possible. In other countries such banks have proved a great success, and they will certainly do as well, if not better, here. .

[Port Huron (Mich.) Times, November 29, 1890.]

Postmaster-General Wanamaker, in his annual report, just published, recommends a new plan for postal-savings banks, the interest to be paid depositors to be filed by the Secretary of the Treasury at the beginning of each year, and to be one-half of 1 per cent. less than the average rate paid to depositors by private bankers, all postal savings to be deposited in the national banks on application. The Secretary also believes it will be for the interest of the postal service to have an ocean mail service.

[Leavenworth (Kans.) Times, November 24.]

POSTAL SAVINGS BANKS.

Postmaster-General Wanamaker has much faith in postal savings banks, and he will give evidence of it in his forthcoming annual report. He believes that one of the secrets of the causes of there not being money in circulation lies in the fact that in many sections of the country millions of dollars are secreted under carpets, in bed clothing, and elsewhere, or buried in the ground by persons afraid of the stability of the banking institutions, or who, having but a few dollars, are timid about opening accounts of deposit with banks.—*Atchison Globe.*

[St. Louis Democrat, November 30.]

There is force in the suggestion of Mr. Wanamaker that postal savings banks are particularly desirable in States that have no laws authorizing and regulating savings banks. Missouri is such a State, and her people would certainly be benefited by a system of banks adapted to the uses of the working classes.

[Toledo Blade, December 1, 1890.]

He also recommends postal savings banks, and outlines briefly his plan. A similar system has been in operation in Great Britain for a number of years, and has proved very successful. The only objection that is raised against it here is the general one that the Government should keep its hands off everything which is not purely governmental, and that paternalism is to be avoided in any and every guise.

[Tacoma Ledger, December 1, 1890.]

The suggestion of Postmaster-General Wanamaker, in his annual report, that the Post-Office Department go into a savings-bank business is worth considering. The suggestion is by no means new. It has its objections and they have been frequently quoted and fully discussed. There is this to be said in favor of the proposition, however, that if such a system of savings banks could be established, and so honestly and judiciously conducted as to both gain and retain the confidence of the people, they would do much to prevent the stringencies in the money market which so often and so seriously depress and disarrange business. They would keep in circulation and in use a large amount of money which now lies idle in small sums in the clocks and stockings of the poorer classes. These amounts, though small, are so numerous that they aggregate many millions of dollars. If this money could be kept in active use, as it would be if this postal savings bank system could be put into successful operation, it would greatly stimulate business and hasten development much more rapidly than it can otherwise be hastened by any Government arrangement of the circulating medium.

[Winchester (Pa.) Republican, December 3, 1890.]

Postmaster-General Wanamaker shows by his annual report of this year that his earnest desire for the establishment of postal savings banks is in no degree abated. In fact the head of the Postal Department is an enthusiast on this point, and as he is a man of large experience in business affairs, and seems to have given the matter a great deal of time and thought, his views deserve to be carefully studied. We quote his general plan, which is based upon the system as adopted in Canada and England.

Whenever postal savings banks have been introduced they have produced most excellent effect. They have been the means of inducing thousands of persons in the humbler ranks of life to save their earnings. So long as there was no opportunity to put their moderate savings where they would be safe, and at the same time earn something in the way of interest, they were squandered as rapidly as they were received. But no sooner were these postal banks established than thousands hurried to them with their small sums, ranging from a few cents to sums of five dollars or more. They have also shown that once this habit of saving has been introduced it grows rapidly. There has been a large, steady increase throughout Great Britain ever since the experiment was introduced. The sums at present in these depositories amounts to many millions of dollars, and it is safe to say that but for this opportunity offered to these people the greater part of this money would have been spent in ways that would have done more harm than good.

[Grand Forks (Dak.) Plaindealer, December 3, 1890.]

As the Plaindealer has been advocating the establishment of postal savings banks we give what the Postmaster-General has to say on the subject:

"I recommend that the Post-Office Department be authorized to establish postal savings banks under regulations formulated by the Postmaster-General ; that the said banks be located as follows:

"(1) In States having no laws regulating savings banks.

"(2) In any other upon petition of a considerable number of residents of any one locality ; and

"(3) Not more numerously than one post-office for every 10 miles of area ; that the interest to be paid depositors shall be fixed by the Secretary of the Treasury at the beginning of the year, and that one-half of 1 per cent. less than the average rate paid to depositors by private bankers; that all postal savings received within a State shall be placed on deposit with the national banks of that State, on application, in such amounts and at such interest as the Secretary of the Treasury shall prescribe, and that all such deposits be declared by special enactment preferred claims against the banks holding them."

POSTAL SAVINGS BANKS.

5 55

[Bethlehem (Pa.) Times, December 3, 1800.]

The proposed plan of Postmaster-General Wanamaker for the establishment of postal savings banks is sure to call forth a variety of comment. It is very reasonably argued by its critics that the post-office has no right to go into the banking business, and that the scheme is constitutionally unwarranted. This objection may or may not hold good in the day when the plan is put to the test; but it is the cause and not the method of Mr. Wanamaker's suggestion that is of most importance. His argument that much of the present financial stringency is due to the practice that obtains among ignorant people of hoarding their earnings instead of trusting them to the banks is a very sound one. The only way to alter this condition is to educate it out of existence, and there is no better source of education than in the multiplication of small savings stations in all parts of the country.

Whether the postal savings bank is the most practical means is at least questionable. The school bank certainly hits wide of the desired mark. But some means or other should be introduced in every community to induce the working people and those of small means to lay by wealth by driblets, a nickel here and a dime there and once in a while a quarter dollar. The rapidly-increased building associations have accomplished an excellent work in late years in encouraging men and women to "save the pieces" instead of wasting them frivolously. The dime savings banks of various natures have also done much. But the chief difficulty that hampers these and the real reason that so much hard-earned money is treasured up by untaught people is their lack of faith in every person and everything save themselves and their own strong box.

It has been argued that postal savings banks would obviate the trouble, since everybody trusts the Government. But we know many persons who don't. To those who have not been properly taught every agency that reaches out after their money is an artful schemer. It will require much teaching to bring them to another belief, but the establishment of many means for saving and the proof of their soundness will in due course dispel this unfortunate mistrust in banks. Until, however, there shall be, in city and country, accessible to all, some such inducement to economy as those here mentioned the present stringency may be at any time liable to recur.

[Indianapolis Journal, December 4, 1890.]

The New York Sun copies Postmaster-General Wanamaker's suggestion for postal-savings banks, and says:

"This is a very pretty scheme, but will the Postmaster-General be kind enough to point out any provision in the Constitution which permits his Department or any other department of the Federal Government to go into the savings-bank business?"

Will the Sun be kind enough to point out any special provision in the Constitution which authorizes the Government to go into the money-order business, the postal-note business, the postage-stamp or the stamped-envelope business? Without reference to the merits of the suggestion for post-office savings banks, there is as much authority in the Constitution for that as there is for any of the other things named. The Constitution was not intended to prevent progress, though that is about the only use the Democratic party makes of it.

[St. Paul Globe, December 4.]

The Postmaster-General, in his annual report, gives considerable attention to the scheme of postal-savings banks. It has more to commend it than the postal telegraph, and as the official mind discerns the error of his party platform in favoring one-cent letter postage for any early period, this postal-savings-banks scheme is, perhaps, the most hopeful of the several new methods he would attach to the service. Jay Gould speaks of the many millions of dollars that came to light in a recent financial crisis as coming from stockings and household seclusions. Wanamaker believes that there are vast amounts tucked about domestic depositories all over the country, lacking the conveniences of banks or having insufficient faith in their security. These very largely, he supposes, would seek the opportunities afforded by the Government in the postal department. The operation of this system in England has had a salutary influence in promoting economy and prudence among the working classes and people of small earnings. The statement is made that no class of wage-earners in the world are as thrifty as those in New England, and much of the credit is attributed to the savings-bank system. It is not claimed that their earnings average higher than elsewhere, but that the constant invitation to frugality and safe investment is a persuasion that leads to such substantial results. The frequency of towns and villages and the density of population probably enable the private savings banks to meet most of the needs. This is, or may be, the case generally in the larger towns of the country, but a great majority of the population is not convenient to these. The proposition is to establish this department at every post-office where the people petition for it. The Government takes the little sums as they are gathered and pays a small interest. This would evidently be a very valuable economic educational process. The young people would be ambitious to be among the creditors of the Government and acquire habits that will be very useful to them in life.

[Duluth (Minn.) Times, December 4.]

Postmaster-General Wanamaker advises the establishment of the postal savings-bank system in this country. It is something of a surprise that the Government had not provided for such banks several years ago. They would be of inestimable benefit and convenience to the people, in all smaller towns especially. The United States and Germany are the only two great powers which have not in existence this system, which has been so successful in England and other countries. There is little good reason why Congress should not pass an act providing for the addition of this system to our Postal Department.

[Erie (Pa.) Times, December 5, 1890.]

Postmaster-General Wanamaker, in his late confessedly excellent annual report, recommends the establishment of postal savings banks. He had abundant warrant for this recommendation. Such banks have been introduced in England and Canada with beneficial effects. They have been the means of inducing thousands in the humbler ranks of life to accumulate small earnings. So long as there was no opportunity to put their moderate savings where they would be secure and at the same time earn something in the way of interest, they were squandered as rapidly as they were received. But since the establishment of postal banks, thousands have deposited in them in sums ranging from a few cents to $5 or more. The amount at present in the banks reaches many millions, and it can truly be said that but for the chance thus afforded the largest portion would have been expended in ways that would have done more harm than good.

Many persons are disinclined to place their money in the ordinary banks, sound and reliable as those now doing business in Erie have proved. Moreover, the latter do not care to receive very small amounts. It is, it seems to us, greatly to be desired that Congress make the necessary provision for putting the project into operation on at least a small scale.

[Halifax (Pa.) Gazette, December 5.]

The plea which the Postmaster-General makes in his annual report in behalf of post-office savings banks ought to receive attention from Congress. In Great Britain postal-savings banks have been in operation with most satisfactory results for many years. In this country the subject has been frequently brought to the notice of Congress in reports from the Post-Office Department, but up to this time nothing further has been accomplished. It is time something was done. In the light in which the Postmaster-General puts the subject there is no doubt that the system as he proposes it would be a great promoter of thrift among the people. Let Congress do something with this question and not continue to ignore it as has been done in the past.

[Peabody (Mass.) Press, December 6.]

Postmaster-General Wanamaker seems to be a enthusiast on the subject of postal-savings banks and is doubtless in a position to put his theory into experimental practice. He does not favor a system that will encroach upon the field already held by the bankers and consequently will not antagonize the private banking institutions in the country. Neither would he have them infringe upon the established rights of savings institutions and building loan associations.

He believes that postal-savings banks would be a blessing to the common people whose earnings are easily dissipated in the unnecessary as well as the necessary things of life, and that their existence would incite them to the habit of saving by the convenience with which it can be done. Then he believes that there is a class of people who do save but who hoard their savings in all kinds of strange and out of the way places and that the business world suffers because these hoards of money, which he believes aggregate millions, are out of circulation and dead to their intended purpose and general usefulness. Thus he sees in his plan a means to encourage people to thrifty and forehanded habits, and to help the world by the legitimate use of the circulating medium provided by Government for the benefit of the whole people.

He would have the people petition the Post-Office Department for deposit facilities in connection with the local office, and thus the requirement and needs of the community would bring about the post-office savings institutions and it would be literally a peoples' bank, with "Uncle Sam," with all his vast and wonderful resources, as the custodian, investor, and responsible treasurer of the money.

This scheme of Postmaster Wanamaker is most certainly feasible. It is not original with him. The idea has often been presented and many men have made it a pet theory in the years gone by. To put it into successful operation will make some man's name an honorable one. It may as well be Postmaster Wanamaker as another to win this distinction. Something of the kind is to be evolved in this nation without a doubt.

[Mount Joy (Pa.) Herald, December 6.]

Postmaster Wanamaker, in his last report, recommends postal savings banks, as well as postal telegraphs, for our country. Postal-savings banks are especially beneficial to the working classes, and the wonder is that America did not take the lead in establishing them. Even Japan has them since 1875, and her working people deposit over $20,000,000 a year into them for interest and safe keeping. By all means let us have postal-savings banks.

[Lansingburgh (N.Y.) Times, December 6, 1890.]

Penny savings institutions are to be established in Boston on a plan essentially the same as the British postal savings bank. The purpose is to afford the poor a convenient means of saving small sums. No interest will be paid, as the income from such investments as can be made will not be larger than the expense of handling the funds. The benefits to be derived from the system are largely more than the money that can be saved. That is not likely in any case to grow into a sum sufficient to more than tide the depositor over some short period of misfortune. The inculcation of the habit of saving is the important thing. It develops thrift and is the surest way of checking pauperism. The person who learns to save has learned the first lesson of success. All the knowledge that can be gained from schools and colleges is not, to the person who must be self-dependent, worth as much as knowledge of how to save and the habit of doing it. It is the foundation of all fortunes. It is the best safeguard against intemperance and immorality. Throughout the world it will be found that, in those countries where there is frugality, there is also the highest average of morality.

[Peabody (Mass.) Reporter, December 6.]

Postmaster-General Wanamaker seems to be an enthusiast on the subject of postal savings banks, and is doubtless in a position to put his theory into experimental practice. He does not favor a system that will encroach upon the field already held by the bankers, and consequently will not antagonize the private banking institutions in the country. Neither would he have them infringe upon the established rights of savings institutions and building loan associations.

He believes that postal savings banks would be a blessing to the common people whose earnings are easily dissipated in the unnecessary as well as the necessary things of life, and that their existence would incite them to the habit of saving by the convenience with which it can be done. Then he believes that there is a class of people who do save, but who hoard their savings in all kinds of strange and out-of-the-way places, and that the business world suffers because these hoards of money, which he believes aggregate millions, are out of circulation and dead to their intended purpose and general usefulness. Thus he sees in his plan a means to encourage people to thrifty and forehanded habits, and to help the world by the legitimate use of the circulating medium provided by Government for the benefit of the whole people.

He would have the people petition the Post-Office Department for deposit facilities in connection with the local office, and thus the requirements and needs of the community would bring about the post-office savings institution and it would be literally a peoples' bank, with "Uncle Sam," with all his vast and wonderful resources, as the custodian investor, and responsible treasurer of the money.

This scheme of Postmaster Wanamaker is most certainly feasible. It is not original with him. The idea has often been presented, and many men have made it a pet theory in the years gone by. To put it into successful operation will make some man's name an honorable one. It may as well be Postmaster Wanamaker as another to win this distinction. Something of the kind is to be evolved in this nation without a doubt.

[Pottsville (Pa.) Journal.]

Postmaster-General Wanamaker in his annual report again calls attention to his favorite scheme of postal savings banks. Mr. Wanamaker's general plan is based upon the system adopted in Canada and England. He proposes that the Post-Office Department be authorized to establish savings banks, under regulations to be formulated by the Postmaster-General, and that they be located first, in States having no laws regulating savings banks; and second, in any other State upon petition of a considerable number of residents of any one locality.

Mr. Wanamaker further suggests that they be not more numerous than one for every 10 miles of area; that the interest to be paid depositors shall be fixed by the Secretary of the Treasury at the beginning of the year, and that it be one-half of 1 per cent. less than the average paid to depositors by private bankers. He also recommends that all postal savings received within a State shall be placed on deposit with the national banks of that State on application, in such amounts and at such interest as the Secretary of the Treasury shall prescribe. All such deposits are to be delared by special enactment preferred claims against the banks holding them.

There is no doubt that a system of banking which invites small payments would be of incalculable benefit to thousands of persons in the humbler walks of life. The tendency with the poorer classes of people is to spend everything because their monthly savings are at the most so meager that they appear hardly worth putting aside. Experience has shown that these same people will deposit in a postal savings bank sums so small that they would never think of carrying to an ordinary bank. In Great Britain, where postal savings banks have been in existence for some years, the deposits amount to many millions and range from a few cents up to hundreds of dollars. The existence of the banks has taught the people the value of caring for the pennies and having the pounds care for themselves.

The general notion that these banks can flourish only at the cost of the banks now in existence is disapproved by the experience in the countries already named. It has there been found not only that the most of the patrons of the penny banks were not patrons of the other banking houses, but that when once they have learned the art of saving, they speedily transfer their accounts to the other banks. Their reasons for this are twofold, the larger banks pay a higher rate of interest, and the depositors naturally desire to become identified with the bigger concerns for very obvious reasons. With this usual foresight, Mr. Wanamaker has taken care that his plan shall endeavor to stimulate this thrift, and at the same time point the people to the larger banks as those which still pay the higher rates of interest.

[Keyser (W. Va.) Echo, December 12.]

Several countries have adopted the postal-savings-bank system, and the success has been such as warrants imitation. Postmaster-General Wanamaker recommends the introduction of postal-savings banks, with such conditions that they ought to prove helpful to the people and also to other savings banks. Let us have the postal-savings bank.

[Newport (R. I.) News, December 12.]

Postmaster-General Wanamaker not only advises penny postage, but recommends the establishment of postal-savings banks throughout the country. * * *

That there are numerous difficulties in engrafting the savings-bank system on the Post-Office Department is evident, but they are not too great to be overcome, providing an improved civil service is adopted in the matter of appointments to office. It may be urged with a show of truth that if such a system of savings banks could be established, and so honestly and judiciously conducted as to both gain and retain the confidence of the people, they would do much to prevent the stringencies in the money market which so often and so seriously depress and disarrange business. They would keep in circulation and in use a large amount of money which now lies idle in small sums in the clocks and stockings of the poorer classes. These amounts, though small, are so numerous that they aggregate many millions of dollars. If this money could be kept in active use, as it would be if this postal-savings-bank system could be put into successful operation, it would greatly stimulate business and hasten development much more rapidly than it can otherwise be hastened by any Government arrangement of the circulating medium. Nevertheless, it is a subject not to be readily disposed of, and the objections that may be urged are of the most weighty character.

[Philadelphia Bulletin, December 12.]

Mr. Wanamaker's postal savings banks scheme is progressing in the Senate, which has instructed the Post-Office Committee to inquire into its advisability. There has been some opposition to it manifested in popular discussion, but it has been mostly in Democratic papers, and the general tone of public opinion seems to favor it. A great deal will depend, however, on the details of its disposition and management.

[Milford (Mass.) Gazette.]

The advocates of a postal savings bank system find a strong argument in the experience of Japan, where such a system has been in existence for the past 15 years. The object is to encourage thrift among people of moderate means, and the accomplishment of that object is seen in the fact that in the first year there were 2,000 depositors with over $15,000 to their credit, while last year's report shows that in Tokio alone, $10,400,000 had been deposited by 356,000 persons, while the total amount of deposits throughout Japan exceeded $20,000,000.

[Parker (Pa.) Phœnix, December 26.]

The postal savings banks are being introduced into several countries, they have proven extremely successful in England and now benighted Japan has taken a step ahead of this highly civilized and progressive country and adopted the postal savings bank feature. It is the poor man's depository, for it is controlled by the Government, consequently safe. The difference of 1 or 2 per cent. to the laboring man is nothing in comparison to the knowledge that his savings are perfectly secure. The want of a savings institution is mostly felt in small manufacturing towns.

[Bloomington (Ill.) Leader, December 29.]

The Postmaster-General, in view of the increasing demand for savings opportunities, is urging upon Congress the enactment of a law establishing a postal savings system. He recommends the establishment of postal savings banks in States having no laws regulating savings banks or in other States upon petition of a certain number of residents of any one locality.

These banks are to be located at the post-offices and be placed in charge of the postmaster, and shall not be nearer to each other than one for every 10 miles of area. He proposes that interest be paid to depositors at one-half of 1 per cent. less than the average rate paid to depositors by private bankers, and that the money deposited in these postal banks shall be placed on deposit with the national banks of the State in which the deposit is made at such interest as the Secretary of the Treasury shall prescribe, making all such deposits preferred claims against the banks holding them. This proposition meets generally the approval of those who have made a study of the savings-banks system. The chief objection to postal savings banks in the past has been that they would take the money out of circulation, as no plan heretofore presented had provided for the loaning or handling of the funds so deposited. Of course the secret of success of any bank is in the fact that it handles over and over again the money deposited with it by its customers, making itself responsible for the money so that it can be paid at any time even although loaned out to somebody else. The objection to the postal banks saving system heretofore has been that no provision was made for keeping this money so deposited in circulation.

The plan proposed, however, by the Postmaster-General, it is believed, obviates this, and will have the double value of supplying a low rate of interest to depositors and at the same time keeping the money in circulation. The objection has also been urged that the Government could not afford to pay interest to depositors, but this plan, which proposes the reloaning of funds to national banks, will of course require those banks to pay as high a rate of interest at least as the Government pays to depositors, and will at the same time continue the money in circulation. Mr. Wanamaker's plan is commented upon by those who have made a study of the financial question as a very ingenious and practicable one, which, combined with the systems in use in other countries, would be extremely valuable in the United States. The postal savings-bank system of Great Britain continues to give great satisfaction there. Over 8,000,000 people made deposits last year with the postal savings banks of that country, their total deposits for the year being in rounds numbers $100,000,000. In France the postal savings deposits amount to over $53,000 and in Belgium over $50,000.

[Salem (Mass.) Register, January 1, 1891.]

All the post-offices in Italy receive money on deposit, at the rate of 3½ per cent. And why shouldn't the post-offices in the United States do the same thing ? In localities in which savings banks abound there is no necessity for the Government to receive deposits ; but the post-offices abound all over the country, and in every section there are people who would gladly avail themselves of the privilege of saving their money through the postal banks.

[Chicago News, January 3.]

Recent failures of private banking institutions in Chicago serve to emphasize, by their revelations of irresponsible banking methods, the need of greater security for small depositors.

Postal savings banks are wanted. This nation is the only one of importance, except Germany, that has not encourgaged the thrift of its citizens by taking care of their small savings. In Great Britain and her colonies, France, Belgium, the Netherlands, Sweden, and even the Hawaiian Kingdom, the postal savings bank is an institution of incalculable benefit to persons of small means but thrifty habits. The accumulation of small savings in most of these countries has increased at such a rate since the establishment of postal savings banks as to form a total of enormous magnitude. The beneficence of the system is unquestioned ; it enables the savings of small depositors to be taken care of at a minimum cost. The postal savings banks are not money-making institutions. Like the postal service, the Government endeavors to serve the people at actual cost. There is greater security than can be possible in the best of private banks, as the national credit is pledged to every depositor. This absolute security undoubtedly accounts for the success of the system wherever tried, even in spite of the fact that the Government always offers a lower rate of interest than banks under private control.

But perhaps the greatest argument in favor of postal savings banks is the fact that they bring banking facilities within easy reach of all classes of the people and in every section of the nation. This argument is skillfully employed by Postmaster-General Wanamaker, who is an enthusiastic advocate of these banks. In his last annual report Mr. Wanamaker says:

"It is not the large cities that feel this need, though even at the populous centers banking institutions generally do not offer convenient hours for working people and do not care to deal with small sums. It is the large mass of wage-earners outside of large cities that clamor for help to keep hard-earned gains. In some of the States no laws exist to give State protection to savings deposited with private capitalists. It is stated on reputable authority that in one portion of the country containing 12,000,000 of population there are not as many places of deposit for the savings of small sums as exist in a single city of 80,000 people in a New England State."

Mr. Wanamaker's recommendation is that postal savings banks should be located "(1) in States having no laws regulating savings banks; (2) in any other State upon petition of a considerable number of residents of any one locality, and (3) not more numerously than one post-office for every 10 miles of area." The Postmaster-General has also outlined in his report the working details of such a system. The obvious advantage to be gained in the initial establishment of such banks is that the working machinery is ready at hand. United States post-offices would simply have a savings-bank annex. The immense advantage to depositors of having their savings where panics would not affect them nor the danger of ordinary banking discourage increased thrift is so obvious that the people should unite in a demand for postal savings banks.

[Troy (Pa.) Register, January 3, 1891.]

Penny savings institutions are to be established in Boston on a plan essentially the same as the British postal-savings bank. The purpose is to afford the poor a convenient means of saving small sums. No interest will be paid, as the income from such investments as can be made will not be larger than the expense of handling the funds. The benefits to be derived from the system are largely more than the money that can be saved. That is not likely in any case to grow into a sum sufficient to more than tide the depositor over some short period of misfortune. The inculcation of the habit of saving is the important thing. It develops thrift and is the surest way of checking pauperism. The person who learns to save has learned the first lesson of success. All the knowledge that can be gained from schools and colleges is not, to the person who must be self dependent, worth as much as knowledge of how to save and the habit of doing it. It is the foundation of all fortunes. It is the best safeguard against intemperance and immorality. Throughout the world it will be found that, in those countries where there is frugality, there is also the highest average of morality.

[Keokuk (Iowa) Gate City, January 10, 1891.]

Postmaster-General Wanamaker is an enthusiastic advocate of postal-savings banks, a public system of saving that has been encouraged in many European countries with marked success. He says:
" It is not the large cities that feel this need, though even at the populous centers banking institutions generally do not offer convenient hours for working people and do not care to deal with small sums. It is the large mass of wage-earners outside of large cities that clamor for help to keep hard-earned gains. In some of the States no laws exist to give State protection to savings deposited with private capitalists. It is stated on reputable authority that in one portion of the country containing 12,000,000 of population there are not as many places of deposit for the savings of small sums as exist in a single city of 80,000 people in a New England State."
These banks could be established in the post-offices as an annex and conducted at an additional expense that would be comparatively small. Depositors would be assured of the safety of their deposits. Monetary panic, financial crises, and mercantile convulsions would not affect their absolute security.

[Aurora (Ill.) Democrat, January 16.]

The recent failure of several private banking institutions, as that of Kean & Co., at Chicago, calls attention to the need of greater security for small depositors, and in considering this question what is more practical than the postal-savings bank system, the establishment of which was so earnestly urged on Congress by the Postmaster-General in his recent report ? Among the strongest arguments in favor of this system is the fact that it will bring banking facilities within easy reach of all classes of the people and in every section of the nation. Postal-savings banks are not money-making institutions. Like the postal service, the Government endeavors to serve the people at actual cost. There is greater security than can be possible in the best of private banks, as the national credit is pledged to every depositor. No doubt this absolute security accounts for the success of the system wherever tried, although the Government pays a lower rate of interest than banks under private control. In his report Postmaster-General Wanamaker says on this subject:
It is not the large cities that feel this need, though even at the populous centers banking institutions generally do not offer convenient hours for working people and do not care to deal with small sums. It is the large mass of wage-earners outside of large cities that clamor for help to keep hard-earned gains. In some of the States no laws exist to give State protection to savings deposited with private capitalists. It is stated on reputable authority that in one portion of the country containing 12,000,000 of population there are not as many places of deposit for the savings of small sums as exist in a single city of 80,000 people in a New England State.
The Postmaster-General's recommendation is that postal-savings banks should be located " in States having no laws regulating savings banks, in any other State upon petition of a considerable number of residents of any one locality, and not more numerously than one post-office for every 10 miles of area." The advantage to be gained in the initial establishment of such banks is that the working machinery is ready at hand. United States post-offices would simply have a savings-bank annex. The immense advantage to depositors of having their savings where panics would not affect them nor the danger of ordinary banking discourage increased thrift must be obvious to every thinking person. The subject is one which certainly demands the most earnest consideration of Congress.

[Wilkes Barre (Pa.) Record, January 19, 1891.]

One of the most unfortunate results of the consolidation of our city schools is the breaking up of the school-savings system introduced by Superintendent Potter, by permission of the directors of the third district school board. Mr. Potter had spent much time in studying the merits of the school-savings system as in practice in other wideawake cities, had convinced the directors of the third district that the schools here presented a fine field for its introduction, and by their permission he had set the system in operation here, so modified as to excellently meet the requirements of our people. Though in operation for but a few months, the usefulness and complete success of the idea were fully demonstrated. Pupils quickly took up with the idea, and hundreds who had never thought of saving at once took in the lesson in thrift and had the pleasure of seeing their pennies accumulate and form dollars. The parents who at first, perhaps, distrusted the innovation soon viewed it with great favor and the teachings of the schoolroom extended to the wider sphere of the home. Older persons than pupils received their first ideas of economy and saving, and the result was highly beneficial to a considerable number.

Unfortunately, with the consolidation of the schools under one management, Mr. Potter's system, planned for one district, was found impracticable in its application to the schools of the entire city under existing conditions, and its operations ceased at the close of the last school year. During the current year no deposits have been received and the books have been returned to the children, who have in many instances drawn out their little accounts and spent the money accumulated. In a number of instances, however, the children have continued to make deposits with the bank, hoarding their pennies and nickels at home until they made up the dollar, the smallest sum the banks receive. In nearly every instance where the books have been returned to the parents regret has been freely expressed that the system should have been abandoned, and there is every evidence that it was popular with the patrons of the schools to a degree that strongly urges its restoration in some form.

The system introduced was discarded because it required the service of some one official in gathering the weekly deposits and having them properly accredited, and no such official, with the time at his disposal, can be found in our school department. The entering of weekly deposits of a few cents each on the accounts of so many as are included in our entire school system seemed also too great an undertaking for the banks, especially as the deposits would be made by the teachers. No modification of the system has yet been suggested that seemed practical. In this emergency we would call attention to what is called the "stamp system," put into operation in Baltimore by the Provident Savings Bank, not for school children, but for the general public. The system has proved so eminently successful that it is being introduced in New York, Boston, Detroit, St. Paul, Denver, San Francisco, and other cities. Indeed, so widely are its merits recognized that a large bank supply house in New York is prepared to furnish all the books, blanks, stamps, etc. The Provident Savings Bank began to offer facilities for small depositors, first by establishing branch offices in twenty or thirty places in the city where deposits could be made on Saturday nights. The business grew rapidly and the rush became so great that the work of entering in bank books and ledgers the many small sums became too great. The bank then began searching for some simpler and more expeditious system, and on the suggestion of Dr. Remsen, of Johns Hopkins University, adopted the stamp-system.

The plan, briefly outlined, is this: Supplies of stamps, signature cards and depositors' cards are left with the agencies each week. Any person wishing to become a depositor signs a signature card for identification, and receives for his deposit, if it be less than $5, stamps to the value of his money. These he affixes to the stamp card which also bears his signature. In making further deposits he has but to buy at the agencies more stamps which are also pasted upon the stamp card. When the stamp card contains stamps amounting to $5 it is deposited at the bank, the amount credited to the depositor in the usual bank book, and the stamps are canceled. To make further deposits he gets another card and buys stamps as before. The stamps are somewhat like postage stamps and of three denominations, 5, 10, and 25 cents. It is plain that this system, if introduced here, would find eager patrons. To introduce it into our schools the amount of stamps required on each card might be reduced to $1. A given amount in stamps would be left with each teacher on the first of the week or monthly, the collector on his next trip collecting the money and the unsold stamps and leaving again the usual supply of stamps. This would remove all necessity for the keeping of accounts except with depositors of $1, which could readily be entered by the collector in his rounds. Thus simplified the system could be readily introduced to the great advantage of the community and to the profit of the bank undertaking it.

[St. Joseph (Mo.) Herald, January 21.]

Postmaster-General Wanamaker in his annual report advocates the establishment of postal savings banks wherever there are not sufficient State savings banks and where there are savings banks, if a reasonable number of persons petition therefor. He reasons at considerable length, and the following argument contains some of his best arguments:

To teach economy and thrift as leading up to better citizenship falls short if there is no adequate provision for the safe-keeping of savings. Such places ought to be within an hour's walk of the home of every workingman. They can not be left to private capitalists to provide, because it would not pay them to deal in small sums or perform the necessary labor. The post-offices and the postmasters are in every respect rightly situated to do this work. It would be a great comfort to the people to have these banks that could not be affected in times of financial panic.

The most prolific source of bank failures and the consequent great loss to depositors is the system of deposits as now conducted. A very large portion of the loans made by banks is of money deposited by their customers, and a financial crisis causes a run on the banks that embarrasses them. The strong argument of Mr. Wanamaker is on this point, for confidence in the postal savings banks would never fail and panics from that cause would cease.

These postal savings banks are not intended to take deposits on running accounts against which checks may be promiscuously drawn, but only time deposits are taken and are not suited for the everyday deposits of business men, and on these time deposits interest is paid.

Of all the great powers only Germany and the United States are without postal savings banks, and in all the countries where they are in use they have proven entirely safe and very popular. Great Britain's postal banks had last year 8,101,120 depositors, an increase of more than half a million, with deposits amounting to $100,000,000. Even in Ireland the increase of deposits was $457,915.

The postal banks do not take the money out of circulation as it is deposited in banks. Mr. Wanamaker recommends that the deposits be made in national banks, and by special enactment be made preferred claims. This would make the deposits safe and would prevent embarrassments to banks by runs brought on by financial scares.

General Wanamaker is a reformer, one among ten thousand, who is able and willing to stand firm against the interests that always block the ways to reforms. Such men as he and Secretary Rusk are in demand, and none other can save us from the fate of the Roman republic. Our Government has become a machine of oppression by which the masses are robbed and the classes enriched, and if we have any desire to transmit to posterity a Government worth preserving, it is full time for an awakening to the perils that surround us. The most effective means we can employ is to support such men as Rusk and Wanamaker.

[Kansas City Journal, January 23, 1891.]

The Postmaster-General's report recently published contains probably the strongest showing that can be made in favor of a postal savings system. Mr. Wanamaker's statements of fact may be relied upon, though the public will of course draw their own conclusions as to whether, upon the showing made, postal savings banks ought to be established in this country.

The system has been adopted, according to Mr. Wanamaker, by all the great powers of the world, except Germany and the United States. It might be well to ascertain why Germany has not adopted it. According to the last report of the postal authorities of Great Britain an average of one person in every eight of the population is a depositor. In England and Wales the average deposit is $70, and in Ireland $94. A recent French report shows the total amount of deposits in postal savings banks to be about $60,000,000, and in 1888 the Belgium depositors had $50,000,000 to their credit. Even in India there were two years ago 5,966 post-office banks with 261,157 depositors. The Hawaiian Islands have a postal savings system, and the deposits last year amounted to nearly $1,000,000.

Mr. Wanamaker believes that postal-savings banks encourage thrift on the part of people who never think of starting bank accounts now. He does not believe that they would interfere with the present banking system, but would rather be the depositories for the money of people who either do not at present save anything or else hide their savings in cracked tea cups. He would particularly guard against interference with other banks by locating the postal banks as follows: First, in States having no laws regulating savings banks; second, in any other States upon petition of a considerable number of residents of any one locality; and third, not more numerously than one post-office for every 10 miles of area. He would have the interest rate fixed by the Secretary of the Treasury at the beginning of every year, and would make it one-half of 1 per cent. lower than the average rate paid by private bankers. And finally he recommends that all postal savings received within a State should be placed on deposit with the national banks of the State at such rates of interest as the Secretary of the Treasury should prescribe, and should be preferred claims against the banks holding them.

That in brief is Postmaster-General Wanamaker's postal-savings bank scheme which is submitted for the approval or rejection of the people.

[Salt Lake City Herald, January 24, 1891.]

In his last annual report Mr. Wanamaker urges the adoption of another scheme which will meet with a more friendly reception, provided the details shall be satisfactory. He advocates the establishment of a system of postal-savings banks, especially at places where there are not sufficient State savings institutions. One of the arguments he employs is contained in the following extract from his report:

"To teach economy and thrift as leading up to better citizenship falls short if there is no adequate provision for the safe-keeping of savings. Such places ought to be within an hour's walk of the home of every workingman. They can not be left to private capitalists to provide, because it would not pay them to deal in small sums or perform the necessary labor. The post-offices and the postmasters are in every respect rightly situated to do this work. It would be a great comfort to the people to have these banks that could not be affected in times of financial panic."

Many of the leading nations of the world have postal-savings banks, and we believe that they everywhere work admirably. This is certainly true of Great Britain, where there are more than 8,000,000 depositors, and the deposits aggregate a hundred million dollars. The laboring people want a place where they can invest their small savings and know that the money is safe; that they can get their money when they want it, regardless of panics or runs on the banks.

But we can not believe that the plan will be a success in this country, at least for many years to come, and for this reason: The Government can borrow all the money it requires at 2 per cent. interest per annum. Two per cent. Government bonds would to-day fetch a premium, especially if they were long-time bonds. Then, to pay more than that would be bad financiering, and subject the Congress which authorized it to some criticism. On the other hand, savings banks pay from 3 to 6 per cent. interest, according to location and the demand for money. In this city the rate is 5 per cent.; in New York it is from 3 to 4; in San Francisco it is 4; in Washington State it is 6. And so it goes; everywhere the rate being higher than the Government, which has no real use for the money, the income being greater than the expenditures, could pay. How much money would the working people of Salt Lake, or any city or town in Utah, deposit in a postal savings bank which paid 2 or 3 per cent. interest per annum when they could get double the interest in a private savings bank or three or four times the interest by loaning to individuals? The absolute safety which the Government bank would afford might induce the individual to deposit there at a lower rate of interest, but not at a rate less than half of what could be obtained elsewhere.

The postal savings bank will yet, we believe, become popular in this country, as elsewhere, and will prove a great benefit to the laboring classes, but it will not be until the nation is older and the use of money is worth less than at present.

[Indianapolis Journal, January 24, 1891.]

The deposits of the savings banks in New England, New York, Pennsylvania, and New Jersey amounted to $1,279,000,000, according to the reports made for the year 1890—an increase of $65,000,000 over the preceding year. The number of depositors was 3,520,000, an increase of 140,000 during the past year. As the population of those States was 17,300,000, it appears that 1 person in 5 is a depositor. The increase of deposits the past year was over $17 to each depositor, and nearly $4 to each inhabitant. There is no reason why the 45,000,000 inhabitants of the rest of the country should not have saved as much as those of the Eastern States. If the valuation was made in property instead of money the savings in the rest of the country would show a larger aggregate. If they saved three-fourths as much, the annual savings of the wage-earners of the country would be $200,000,000.

The New York Bulletin estimates that the total savings of all those who work for wages and salaries is over $200,000,000 a year. The Western wage-earners do not deposit their savings in savings banks, for the reason that there are few such banks, and more profitable investments are found in hundreds of local loan and building associations. It is very probable that wage-earners in cities like Indianapolis are saving as much money *per capita* as those in the East, for the reason that living is cheaper in the older States of the West than in the East, and the rivalry of the managers of loan associations is greater than that of savings banks. Furthermore, many wage-earners in the smaller towns of the West, when there are no other places of deposit or investment, put their savings in the ordinary business banks. Supposing that the accumulations of the 45,000,000 people in the rest of the country are as large as those of the 17,300,000 in the East, the total of money owned by wage-earners and people of small means can not be less than $2,500,000,000. It may not all be in banks or loan associations, but it is at their call.

Now suppose, in compliance with the demand for more money, Congress should provide for the free coinage of silver or issue fiat paper until the amount outstanding should be equal to $50 per capita, thus depreciating the purchasing power of these savings 20 per cent. or more—what would be the result? Simply this: These wage-earners who have this vast amount of accumulations in savings institutions, loan associations and banks would be as effectually deprived of $500,000,000 as if they had been deprived of it by theft or highway robbery. It would not be so evident a robbery, but it would be as actual. Theories are often delusive, but facts are not; and the facts gleaned from experience prove that when a people resort to a money which is not based upon the coin which the commercial world uses, that money will not have the purchasing power of the money of commerce. To-day the United States has that money. Fifteen years ago we did not have it, and our dollar was worth not over 85 cents in the money of the world, and its purchasing power was less by 15 per cent. Wage-earners should be the last to listen to the clamor about cheap money and free silver coinage.

[Manufacturers' Record, Baltimore, Md., January 24, 1891.

SAVINGS BANKS NEEDED.

Savings banks are institutions in which money can be deposited in small sums and earn an increase. They are not intended for the deposits of investors and capitalists, for they are presumed to be capable of taking care of what they have and of knowing how to employ it to advantage. The savings bank is the custodian of the petty surplus of the poor, the careful savings of self-denial, the spare dollars that would otherwise be spent needlessly, the small legacies belonging to widows and orphans. Their treasury assets represent aggregations of repeated deposits of small sums, few or none of them large enough, singly, to make any showing on the ledger. Some of these banks will open an account for a 1-cent deposit; others have a dime as their least limit; others a dollar, but nearly all refuse to extend accounts beyond $5,000, and much prefer to keep them below that sum. Nor is it the chief aim of savings banks to make as much money as possible. The policy is first to save money; next to add something to it by accumulations of savings and of earnings.

In the truest and best sense savings banks were intended to be institutions of practical benevolence, and whenever they have been conducted on that idea they have been a blessing to their depositors and to the communities in which they were located. Their mode of operation is simple, easily understood, and safe beyond all possiblitiy of serious losses if the managers are competent and honest. An example will illustrate the system. In 1838 the trustees of a recently chartered savings bank in Connecticut announced that their books would be opened for deposits on a certain day. The first to appear at the time specified was a young mechanic, who deposited $10 to the credit of his infant daughter. From time to time, when he had a few dollars to spare, he put them to the same account. Other parents did likewise. Needlewomen, servant girls, wage-earners, children who were influenced by their parents to save a part of their pocket money, farmers with a few dollars for which they had no immediate need, became frequent depositors. Whenever these dimes and dollars aggreated enough of a sum for the purpose, it was loaned on first-class security with a large margin for safety. Every 6 months the net profits of these accumulated savings were distributed pro rata among the depositors, and, unless withdrawn, was placed to their credit and became a part of their capital.

As years passed and population increased, depositors were more and more numerous, and now that bank has more than $7,300,000 to the credit of its 22,579 depositors and a surplus sufficient to make good any possible shrinkage of value in the securities upon which its money is loaned. A remarkable fact in this connection is that fully four of these, more than $7,000,000 represent the savings of servant girls and other small wage-earners.

These banks have been among the chief factors of New England's prosperity. The enormous sums that have gone into railroad, mining, and manufacturing enterprises in the West could never have been spared from New England but for these banks. Their aggregated millions of dollars have been the solid reserve fund from which capitalists could borrow what they needed upon gilt-edge securities. They have supplied manufacturers and merchants with money when they needed it, at times when banks of discount and exchange could not accommodate them. They have furnished the facilities that enabled tens of thousands of thrifty people to own their homes who would otherwise have been rent-payers all their days.

The deposits in the savings banks of New England, New York, New Jersey, and Pennsylvania during 1890 aggregated the enormous sum of $1,279,000,000, an increase over 1889 of $65,000,000. The depositors numbered 3,520,000, a gain of 110,000 for the year. This was equal to a saving of $4 per capita for the 17,300,000 population of those nine States. Referring to these facts, the Pittsburgh Commercial Gazette says:

"These figures show not only that the working classes have been prosperous, but that they have been thrifty as well. The disposition to save has been growing with the opportunities for saving, and the deposits in the savings banks fall far short of exhibiting the full extent of the accumulations. There are scores of building and loan associations, each with hundreds of stockholders, and the weekly contributions in the form of dues foot up millions annually. The shareholders for the most part have for their object the procurement of homes, but many seek this form of investment because it brings a higher interest than is paid by the savings banks. The annual savings in the manufacturing States are certainly largely in excess of. $4 per capita in periods of prosperity, and, taking the whole country through, $250,000,000 would not be an excessive estimate of the annual savings when work is plenty and wages good.

"There are sections of the country in which savings banks are few and far between, and in which the accumulations must necessarily be largely withdrawn from circulation. Money invested in banks does not lie idle, and that which goes into building and loan treasuries is actively employed, but where there are none of these facilities for investment the small hoardings are laid away in a secure corner to meet the purposes for which they are intended."

The South has a few savings banks, and within a few years has organized quite a number of building and loan associations. These latter are useful institutions when confined to home purposes and managed by home people, but when their field of operations is widely extended they are exposed to hazards of various kinds that endanger their safety. Savings banks are very different affairs. They accumulate money that would be stowed away in hiding places until needed. They put it into circulation under safeguards that insure its return to its owners. It is very much within bounds to say that there are now hidden away in the South $50,000,000 in small sums that would be restored to circulation and usefulness if there were savings banks in all the considerable towns of every State.

[Cottage City (Mass.) Herald, February 5.]

On the continually urged subject of savings banks under the Post-Office Department of the Government, the Postmaster-General, in his annual report, says:

"It is the large mass of wage-earners outside of large cities that clamor for help to keep hard-earned gains. To teach economy and thrift as leading up to better citizenship falls short if there is no adequate provision for the safe-keeping of savings. Such places ought to be within an hour's walk of the home of every workingman. They can not be left to private capitalists to provide, because it would not pay them to deal in small sums or perform the necessary labor. The post-offices and the postmasters are in every respect rightly situated to do this work. It would be a great comfort to the people to have these banks that could not be affected in times of financial panic.

"Of all the great powers of the world, the United States and Germany alone are without postal savings systems. The last report of the British authorities shows that on the average 1 person out of every 8 is a depositor, and while in England and Wales the average balance to each depositor is almost $70, in Ireland, where the conditions are harder, the average balance to each depositor is close to $94."

The advantage to the towns and villages of this country, in case of financial panic, can not be estimated, and the thrift and gain from interest to the people will result in an enormous increase in the people's wealth, a great part of which is to-day hidden away in odd places subject to destruction by fire and thieves.

[Manufacturer's Record, Baltimore, February 14, 1891.]

THE SOUTH NEEDS SAVINGS BANKS.

The Manufacturer's Record has persistently sought to impress upon the people of the South the importance of establishing savings banks. No community will develop habits of economy and savings unless encouraged thereto by having a place where every spare dime or dollar can be deposited with absolute safety and with the certainty of drawing a fair rate of interest. With savings banks near at hand every man, woman and child gets into the habit of economizing and putting away a few cents or a few dollars as often as possible in order to prepare for a rainy-day. Where savings banks are not convenient there is but little inducement for the people to make the small savings which gradually aggregate, as in New England, into hundreds of millions of dollars. The South is now producing an enormous amount of wealth; its farmers are prosperous; its laboring classes of all kinds are fully employed at good wages, and with a united effort through the organization of savings associations it would now accumulate surplus wealth more rapidly than any country in the world has ever done. The millions of dollars that are now hid away in old stockings would be drawn out and would furnish an enormous amount of fresh capital with which to handle the business of that section. A compilation from the St. Louis Republic shows the condition of the savings banks in thirty States, containing the number of banks, list of States, estimated population January 1, 1890, number of depositors, aggregate amount of deposits September 30, 1889, amount due each depositor, average due each man, woman and child in the State, and the percentage of depositors to the whole population of each State as follows:

No. of banks	State.	Estimated population, 1890.	No. of depositors.	Total amount of deposits.	Amount due each depositor.	Amount due each person in State.	Per cent. of deposits to its population.
55	Maine...............	660,000	124,562	$40,909,663	$309	$63.00	19
69	New Hampshire....	370,000	145,021	57,300,590	395	155.00	40
31	Vermont	333,000	61,759	17,801,327	288	54.00	17
176	Massachusetts......	2,072.000	983,202	315,135.070	320	153.00	47
38	Rhode Island	330,000	123,102	57,699,884	469	174.00	37
85	Connecticut........	750,000	287,776	105,850,078	267	141.00	38
125	New York	6,500,000	1,362,352	523,077,515	384	80.00	21
13	Pennsylvania.......	5,061,690	213,133	64,968,633	305	13.00	4
25	New Jersey........	1,500,000	114,627	29,696,529	268	20.00	7
2	Delaware	175,000	15,059	3,405.411	230	20.00	8
1	District of Columbia	219,000	11,059	1,154,079	104	5.00	5
20	Maryland...........	1,122,000	122,887	34,203,241	279	30.00	11
1	West Virginia	854,300	1,850	55,123	29	....	....
5	North Carolina.....	1,750,000	5,001	223,801	45	....	
9	South Carolina	1,350,700	13,550	2,692,264	190	2.00	1
7	Georgia............	1,152.700	13,474	1,937,097	61	1.10	2
9	Alabama...........	1,500,000	1,765	236,108	134	....	
1	Louisiana..........	1,030,000	2,889	914,555	319	1.00	....r.....
1	Texas.............	2,190.000	1,069	264,140	247	....	
8	Tennessee	1,800,000	11,734	1,289,527	110	.70	....
11	Ohio	4,000,000	55,109	25,390,712	390	6.35	1½
51	Indiana............	2,440,000	11,606	2,776,119	237	1.00	....
12	Illinois	3,750,060	29,605	7,620,082	257	2.00	3½
56	Michigan	2,250,000	99,245	24,015,207	232	11.00	4
1	Wisconsin	2,000,000	519	47,704	92	....	
50	Iowa	1,875,000	43,609	13,125,058	309	7.00	....
6	Minnesota..........	1,500,000	16,767	3,979,436	237	2.65	1
28	California..........	1,500,000	114,034	87,101,912	764	38.00	8
2	Dakota.............	600,000	434	25,927	56	....	
1	Utah Territory	230,000	6,056	493,276	82	2.13	
849		49,894,300	4,021,523	1,425,230,349	354	29.56	

These figures are worthy of careful study. They show that out of a total population of 2,000,000 in Massachusetts, 983,000 are depositors in savings banks, it being the custom for parents not only to deposit in their own name, but also to make small deposits in the name of every child, so that when their children attain age they may have a start in life. In the savings banks of that State there are $315,000,000, which is more than three times the national banking capital of the whole South, even including Maryland. These $315,000,000 play a greater part in furnishing the capital with which to conduct the business operations of that State than all the national banks in Massachusetts. Even Rhode Island, with 330,000 population, has $57,699,000 in its savings banks. Excluding Maryland, the whole South has less than $10,000,000 in its savings banks.

The leaders in Southern development should consider these facts and endeavor to begin the great work of developing savings banks. There is scarcely a town in the South where a well-managed savings institution could not be made profitable and at the same time prove of much value to the business interests of the place, and encourage in the town, as well as in the surrounding country, habits of thrift and economy. The South will never attain the financial strength which it should have until it learns to concentrate and aggregate its money by means of well-managed savings banks.

[Lafayette (Ind.) Courier, February 21.]

Experience with building and loan associations have demonstrated the fact beyond all question of doubt that they are of inestimable value to the wage-workers of the country and to all others who are ambitious to economize and to provide something for the proverbial rainy day. Well-conducted savings banks are also a boon to those who desire to make small weekly or monthly deposits, but unfortunately there have been so many failures among this class of institutions that their natural patrons have become wary of them—in fact, almost resentful. It should not be understood, however, that these allusions have any bearing upon the Lafayette Savings Bank, whose reputation is beyond criticism. But taking the statistics of the country at large, it will be found that there has been an appalling number of failures of savings banks during the past year, and the tendency has been to create distrust among a class of people who are prone to look upon capitalists as their natural enemies.

The proposition to establish a postal-saving system has been long discussed, but it has never before had the earnest consideration that it is now receiving, and there is a hopeful prospect that the theory will become a substantial reality. By the system, every post-office in the country can be made a safe depository and with the assurance of absolute security. No matter how little confidence the people may have in private institutions, they have firm faith in the integrity of the Government, and will not hesitate nor be afraid to deposit their earnings with the designated and bonded agents of the United States. The system can be established with but comparatively little expense and without increasing the machinery of the Post-Office Department to any appreciable extent. The mechanic or day laborer who would have a feeling of timidity about entering a big banking house to deposit a small share of his earnings, would gladly avail himself of an opportunity to make the deposit with the local postmaster, for the reason that he feels that he has as much right to be there as any other man, for the post-office is a part of the Governmental structure he helps support, and he reckons justly that he is entitled to share in its benefits.

The advantages of the system are manifest and manifold. The first and most important consideration is that the depositor has absolute assurance that there will be no failures, no suspensions, no defalcations that will not be made good by the Government. It will also serve to cultivate a disposition in the direction of economy among a class of people who are most in need of the inculcation of a spirit of that kind, and there is no doubt but that a brief experiment will show most gratifying results. The benefits to be derived from small savings have been demonstrated in the marvelous results achieved by the building and loan associations, and the proposed scheme for a postal-saving system is another long step in the direction of increasing the general comfort and prosperity of the working classes who earn their bread by the sweat of the brow.

[Philadelphia Bulletin.]

Mr. Wanamaker is still a firm believer in postal savings banks, and will advocate them in his forthcoming report. It seems, however, that he would use them as an adjunct to and not a rival of the savings banks of the cities, and would, therefore, establish them principally at county post-offices where there are no other depositories of small sums. No doubt they would be highly useful there.

[Camden (N. J.) Post.]

Postmaster-General Wanamaker shows by his annual report of this year that his earnest desire for the establishment of postal savings banks is in no degree abated. In fact the head of the Postal Department is an enthusiast on this point.

Whenever postal savings banks have been introduced they have produced most excellent effect. They have been the means of inducing thousands of persons in the humbler ranks of life to save their earnings. So long as there was no opportunity to put their moderate savings where they would be safe and at the same time earn something in the way of interest, they were squandered as rapidly as they were received. But no sooner were these postal banks established than thousands hurried to them with their small sums, ranging from a few cents to sums of $5 or more. They have also shown that once this habit of savings has been introduced it grows rapidly. There has been a large, steady increase throughout Great Britain ever since the experiment was introduced. The sums at present in these depositories amounts to many millions of dollars, and it is safe to say that but for this opportunity offered to these people the greater part of this money would have been spent in ways that would have done more harm than good.

[New York Herald.]

Representative Lodge, of Massachusetts, has introduced into the House at Washington a bill for the establishment of postal savings banks.

Such institutions have long been in existence in England, and have there proved highly successful. They have been found to be a great convenience to the masses, and have afforded a sense of security that encourages thrift and promotes industry. There is absolute confidence in the Government, so that when the poor depositor intrusts a dollar to the safekeeping of the Government, he has no shadow of fear that he will not get his dollar back, with interest, whenever he wants it. Moreover, money put in one post-office can be drawn out at any other. For example, if a man has deposited at London he can draw at Liverpool.

But in Boston a voice has already been raised, and in other great municipal centers it will doubtless be raised, against the proposition to introduce the system into this country. The objection is urged that postal savings banks are neither necessary nor desirable. Ample facilities, it is contended, are afforded by existing savings banks which are as secure as human ingenuity and legislation can make them. Their organization and management, investment of deposits, payment of interest, etc., are governed by the most stringent laws. The whole business is subject to a governmental control and supervision so strict that absolute safety is secured. With such a system in successful operation it is claimed that there is no need of postal savings banks, and, moreover, that the establishment of the latter would be absolutely detrimental, because their effect would be to withdraw from the local community the surplus deposits now invested there and transfer them to Washington.

There is force in these views, but it is limited to large cities and towns like those of New England, New York, Pennsylvania and some other States where savings banks are sufficiently numerous for the wants of the people and surrounded with such safeguards as guarantee security. But there are other quarters of the country, notably in the far West and certain parts of the South- and for that matter even rural districts of the North and East—where the objections to postal savings banks do not hold, but where, on the contrary, there are cogent reasons in their favor. Wherever ordinary savings banks are not found or wherever they are not absolutely secure, there a postal savings bank must meet a popular want and serve a useful purpose. There it will afford conveniences and facilities which the people now lack and beget a popular confidence that does not now exist.

We see no reason why these advantages may not be secured without incurring any of the disadvantages urged against the reform. This can easily be done by establishing postal savings banks in those places where they will be a benefit to the people and not establishing them where they are not needed or desired. Indeed, this is practicable under Mr. Lodge's bill, as we understand it, for it empowers the Postmaster-General to designate the offices which shall serve as savings banks. If this power is wisely used the new system can be made a public boon.

UNFAVORABLE.

[Philadelphia Herald, November 25.]

It is said that Postmaster-General Wanamaker will devote considerable space in his forthcoming report to the subject of postal savings banks. It will urge the adoption of such depositories on various grounds, but more particularly because their establishment would promote habits of saving. This is a matter of conjecture, which Mr. Wanamaker permits himself to indulge without reason.

Postal savings banks are objectionable because they bring the Government into competition with individual enterprise on unequal terms. It would be a wise rule to restrain the Government from such competition in all cases. Where individual enterprise fails to meet the public demand for commerce or convenience the Government may properly step in to serve the people. But on no other condition is it permissible.

The tendency is to govern too much. That is the evil effect of Mr. Wanamaker and his party. He and it think that the people are in need of some sort of guardian ship to regulate their lives and their habits. The laws to restrain evil passions and bad tendencies are all right because they are necessary for the protection of the public against the excesses of individuals. But there is just as much need for restraints upon power in its tendency to usurp the functions and absorb the rights of individuals.

This country has no need for postal savings banks. The party in power might be benefited by them, because they would multiply plac-s for party heelers and dependants. But there is no necessity for them from a business standpoint. We have substantial and well-regulated savings banks to accommodate the public, and the trenching on that legitimate business by the Government would be an evil of incalculable magnitude.

[Omaha Herald, November 26.]

Postmaster-General Wanamaker believes that the reason there is a scarcity of money in circulation is due to the fact that millions of dollars are secreted under carpets and in stockings. He is laboring under a serious misapprehension, which is likely to encourage burglars and thugs. It can safely be stated that there is not a man in Omaha who has his carpets padded with $1,000 bank notes, and not a woman who carries $1,000,000 around in the manner that Mr. Wanamaker suspects.

[Boston Globe, November 26.]

Postmaster-General Wanamaker is trying to interest his party in postal savings banks. It would be more to the purpose if the party would stop the McKinley nonsense and give the people a chance to save something. It is easy enough for anybody to find a savings bank; the trouble is to find the savings to put in it.

[San Francisco Bulletin, November 29.]

The establishment of postal savings banks is recommended in States having no laws regulating savings banks, and in others upon application of a considerable number of residents of any one locality; the savings received within a State to be deposited with the national banks in that State on application, in such amount and at such interest as the Secretary of the Treasury may prescribe; such deposits to be declared preferred claims. It is very likely that this proposition will arouse opposition and require amendment. Certainly all other depositors in a national bank would object to letting postal savings banks have the first claim on their deposits in case of a failure. Nor does the plan provide the best security for depositors in the postal banks. National banks do not usually let in their depositors for large losses in case of failure, owing perhaps to Government supervision, but the liability to loss is always present, and a postal savings system should, as far as possible, guaranty against it. If the rule observed in case of Government moneys loaned to national banks, that they be secured by a deposit of bonds in the Treasury, should be made in the case of deposits by postal banks there could be no valid objection from any quarter. Less than that would hardly be satisfactory.

[Philadelphia Record, November 30.]

As for the postal savings bank system, which Mr. Wanamaker again recommends, there is no doubt that it has had some success in European countries which suffer from chronic deficits, and in which banks are held in more or less distrust. But this Government could not pay enough interest to attract depositors without needlessly taking the money out of the Treasury, nor without injuriously competing with the banks. At the same time, it is very questionable whether the national banks would be willing to pay interest on the Government deposits of postal savings while holding large amounts of Treasury money without interest. As a rule, the people of this country are shrewd enough to know where and how to deposit their money, without the kindly aid of a grandfatherly Government.

[Louisville Courier Journal, December 1.]

Furthermore, following the traditional policy of the Republican party, he recommends that the Government shall exercise paternal care over the earnings of the poor and establish for the people a postal savings bank.

The value of savings banks the people themselves are beginning to recognize, and when they have anything to put in them it is quite certain they will be established. Perhaps, if the Government would reduce its expenses and reduce taxation, the farmers and laboring men throughout the West and South might be able to accumulate something and in time establish savings banks of their own. These institutions should be local in character and control. To gather the money of the people and then loan it to the national banks, as Mr. Wanamaker proposes, is unwise. There is no call for this kind of interference by the Government, as the people are perfectly able to take care of these matters themselves.

[New York Sun, December 2.]

Mr. John Wanamaker, Postmaster-General of the United States, in his annual report makes the following recommendation in respect to postal savings banks:

"I recommend that the Post-Office Department be authorized to establish postal savings banks, under regulations formulated by the Postmaster-General. That the said banks be located as follows: (1) In States having no laws regulating savings banks; (2) in any other States, upon petition of a considerable number of residents of any one locality; and (3) not more numerously than one post-office for every 10 miles of area; that the interest to be paid depositors shall be fixed by the Secretary of the Treasury at the beginning of each year, and be one-half of 1 per cent. less than the average rate paid to depositors by private bankers; that all postal savings received within a State shall be placed on deposit with the national banks of that State, on application, in such amounts and at such interest as the Secretary of the Treasury shall prescribe; and that all such deposits be declared by special enactment preferred claims against the banks holding them."

This is a very pretty scheme, but will the Postmaster-General be kind enough to point out any provision in the Constitution which permits his Department or any other department of the Federal Government to go into the savings bank business? Furthermore, can not the people of this country take care of their money without the assistance of the Government? We rather think they can.

The Post-Office Department does not do the work already committed to its charge with such conspicuous success as to convince the people that it ought to be intrusted with a banking business in addition. In this very report of Mr. Wanamaker's he denounces the New York post-office building as totally inadequate to the requirements of the postal service, and says that better quarters are needed; yet it is only a few years ago that this building was put up by a Republican administration at immense expense, and now it is condemned by a Republican Postmaster-General.

We are against any extension of Federal power. To turn every post-office in the land into a savings bank would only tend to strengthen the authority of the Federal officeholders throughout the country. The scheme is of doubtful constitutionality, to say the least, and should be opposed by every Democrat.

[Minneapolis Journal, December 4.]

Postmaster-General Wanamaker's postal-savings-bank scheme does not find very great favor. The public is rather indifferent to it. The fact is, the savings-bank system as operated throughout the country is perfectly satisfactory. There is provision in it for the most minute savings deposits. The Government can't conduct the business better than private concerns can. It is very seldom that a savings bank fails irremediably. Under our State laws they are perfectly safe. The Government has enough to do anyway, without running a savings bank.

[Gordonsville (Va.) Gazette, December 5.]

Postmaster-General Wanamaker recommends the establishment of postal-savings banks all over this broad land. This is another scheme for increasing the Federal power and patronage, and is, we believe, wholly unconstitutional. The people of this country should be able to take care of their own money without interference from the Government. If the Harrison and McKinley crowd should hold the Government for many years, there would be comparatively few persons left in the country with a spare dollar to put in a postal or any other savings bank. If Mr. Wanamaker will drop his wildcat schemes for Government savings banks, parcels post, and telegraph, and will give the public a good mail service, the people will ask nothing more of him.

[Milwaukee News, December 6.]

Postal-savings banks are the hobby of Postmaster-General Wanamaker just now, and he is trying to get his party to indorse the scheme. It would be more to a purpose if the party would stop the high-tariff nonsense and give the people a chance to save something. It is easy enough for anybody to find a savings bank; the trouble is to find the savings to put in it.

[New York Witness, December 10.]

Mr. Wanamaker's proposal to open postal-savings banks wherever called for and to deposit the money lodged in them in the banks of the several States in which the money is received, does not commend itself to our judgment. While the Federal Government was in need of money the Witness again and again urged the opening of post-office savings banks as a means of supplying the Government with funds at a low rate, and at the same time, of offering the people an opportunity for laying by their savings without any risk of loss. But now that the Government has more money than it needs and has no prospect of again requiring to borrow money, except it be on account of very imprudent legislation, we can not see that it would be justified in receiving money on deposit simply to lend it out again. The Government has no more right to go into the banking business than it has to go into the business of raising wheat for market, or of manufacturing shoes.

[Lancaster (Va.) Examiner, December 11.]

Postal-savings banks would probably be a good thing, but there is no great outcry for them at present. When postal-savings banks were established in England, there were in the whole kingdom but twenty savings banks which were open every day; a want remained to be filled. The circumstances are different here.

[Philadelphia Herald, December 12.]

The postal-savings-bank job still stalks forth. In the Senate yesterday it was brought forward and the Post-Office Committee was directed to inquire into the advisability of establishing the scheme. Of course the committee will decide in favor of the banks. The members will no doubt see ample opportunities for them to make profit out of it.

In an interview in Chicago yesterday Mr. Chauncey M. Depew said he didn't believe much in paternal government. That is an additional proof that Mr. Depew has a large and level head. It was by intelligent personal effort that he became the rich and useful man he is. Naturally, therefore, he believes in the Democratic idea of individual effort. "That government is best which governs least."

But the promoters of the postal-savings bank scheme are of a different mind. They believe that the people need to be secured by Government. They imagine that the establishment of postal savings banks will compel people to put their earnings on deposit. It's a silly notion which comes from crazy brains, and the sooner it is abandoned the better.

[San Antonio (Tex.) Express, December 13.]

In the Senate of the United States Mr. Mitchell has introduced a postal-savings bank bill. The scheme is not indorsable, and it will not work. Deposits of money by the people to the credit of the Government have been tried before. It was not the intention of the framers of the Constitution to make the Government rich at the expense of the people. Savings banks inaugurated by private capital have been of great benefit. But a Government savings bank is another matter.

[Omaha Herald, December 28.]

The Postmaster-General is very urgent indeed for the establishment of a postal savings bank, more particularly in places away from centers of population, where people do not enjoy the facilities extended to those who dwell in large cities.

Ill-natured persons might say that the inhabitants of remote rural districts are not so well posted in the world's wicked ways as those who have the opportunity ot perusing the daily papers, but this additional argument is unnecessary for the purposes of this article.

Postal savings banks would undoubtedly prove of great benefit to the people of this country, particularly to those whose means are limited, but who still desire to economize their savings.

But the question arises and presses itself into prominence, whether this is the propitious day and hour for the establishment of these beneficent institutions, which can only be based upon perfect confidence in the unimpeachable integrity of those who are intrusted with their management. And the very ignorance of the common people of the many excellent qualities of Mr. Wanamaker might lead them into error likely to be productive of very serious results—in fact, sufficient to cause the failure of the entire scheme.

[Galveston News, January 18.]

Mr. Wanamaker's postal-savings bank scheme has received the approval of some Democratic papers. On the face of it it seems to be a good thing, that will give security to the poor from bank failures, promote thrift, and cost only a moderate amount for expenses. Let all the advantages be granted, and it still remains to be inquired whether the scheme might not wisely be rejected as part of a system which, among other things, will render the Democratic party obsolete and the system of individual enterprise ultimately impossible. Can it be believed that anyone would be found to advocate paternal measures if these were never demonstrably beneficial either in promoting security or in saving expense? There are many things, perhaps, which the Government can do, if the people so will, in a manner to conserve wealth, increase confidence, and serve the majority of the people, at only the moral cost of striking down some private business and strengthening and widening the trust of the people in the communal powers of Government in industrial matters. But this qualification should be intelligently understood. It bears within itself the main question of the future. It will be hopeless for any party to combat paternalism by combating only its abuses, but claiming its benefits and promoting its introduction wherever it suits themselves.

The hundreds of thousands of people who have read popular works favoring communism know that in conducting the mercantile business of the country so as to avoid the waste in competitive storekeeping and selling goods a prospect has been indicated of a saving far beyond the economy proposed in savings banks; and who shall say that the communistic system, as a whole, depends for trial upon anything else than the acceptance of the principle? It would render savings banks unnecessary if carried out in the fullness of the plan of its latest prominent apostle, Mr. Bellamy. Who will deny that if the Government is to do a banking business for the people because it can displace private banks, the same logic will justify it in doing a mining and manufacturing business, in which it can save the people indefinitely more than through any savings-bank venture? Formerly that sort of experiment was considered as a separate thing. Now the claims of communism come nearer, as a whole, and must be so considered, or else certain parties and classes will find their mistake to be that they have not reckoned with the increase of logical thought in the people. It can not be accepted as a conclusive argument for any plan that it saves some immediate trouble or cost. The more important bearing may be how it turns people into the communistic channel.

[New York Sun, February 7, 1891.]

Mr. Evans, of Tennessee, has introduced into the House of Representatives a bill to establish postal savings banks and encourage small savings. Bills differing more or less from Mr. Evans's in details, but of the same general tenor, have been introduced into previous Congresses. The postal savings bank has become, in fact, a sort of hobby with the benevolent persons who believe in a paternal and do-all Government; and in the South, where savings banks are less common than in the North, the idea has found a certain support among people who are not ordinarily inclined to favor any extension of the power of the Federal Government. The postal savings bank does well enough for England, but that is no reason why it should be introduced into the United States. It is no business of the Government to set up the Post-Office Department as a receiver and guarantor of the savings of citizens, or to impose upon the Secretary of the Treasury and the Postmaster-General, as Mr. Evans's bill provides, the duty of loaning postal savings funds to banks and of issuing interest-bearing certificates of deposit. The business of the Post-Office Department is to carry the mails. The business of the Government is to mind its own business. The citizens of the United States ought to have sense enough to take care of themselves.

www.ingramcontent.com/pod-product-compliance
Lightning Source LLC
Chambersburg PA
CBHW021530270326
41930CB00008B/1185